GOVERNING LOCAL PUBLIC ECONOMIES

GOVERNING LOCAL PUBLIC ECONOMIES

CREATING THE CIVIC METROPOLIS

Ronald J. Oakerson

ICS PRESS

INSTITUTE FOR CONTEMPORARY STUDIES

Oakland, California

To Mom and Dad

This book is a publication of the Institute for Contemporary Studies, a nonprofit, nonpartisan public policy research organization. The analyses, conclusions, and opinions expressed in ICS Press publications are those of the authors and not necessarily those of the Institute or of its officers, its directors, or others associated with, or funding, its work.

Inquiries, book orders, and catalog requests should be addressed to ICS Press, Latham Square, 1611 Telegraph Avenue, Suite 902, Oakland, CA 94612. Tel. (510) 238-5010; Fax (510) 238-8440; Internet www.icspress.com. For book orders and catalog requests, call toll-free in the United States: (800) 326-0263.

Cover and interior design by Rohani Design, Edmonds, WA. Book set in Goudy by Rohani Design and printed and bound by Whitehall Printing Company.

0 9 8 7 6 5 4 3 2 1

Library of Congress Cataloging-in-Publication Data

Oakerson, Ronald J.
    Governing local public economies : creating the civic metropolis / Ronald J. Oakerson.
       p.   cm.
    Includes bibliographical references.
    ISBN 1-55815-512-0 (paper)
    1. Local government—United States. 2. Local finance—United States. 3. County services—Contracting out—United States. 4. Municipal services—Contracting out—United States. 5. Metropolitan areas—United States. 6. Metropolitan government—United States. I. Institute for Contemporary Studies. II. Title.
JS323.O18 1999
352.14'0973—dc21   99–10992
                                                        CIP

CONTENTS

Chapter Two

Chapter Three

Chapter Four

Chapter Five

METROPOLITAN GOVERNANCE—WITHOUT METROPOLITAN GOVERNMENT 80

Chapter Six

THE CIVIC METROPOLIS 106

A NOTE
FROM THE PUBLISHER

IN ADDITION TO OUTLINING A NEW WAY of viewing and analyzing issues of governance and service provision in metropolitan areas, *Governing Local Public Economies* fundamentally challenges the organizational reform tradition of recommending consolidation or regionalization of local governments.

For years scholars and reformers of local government have been seeking the "one best" organizational structure to govern emerging metropolitan areas. Even today, consolidation of local governments into one best structure is the reform favored by many. Instead of regarding metropolitan areas as fragmented systems in need of organization and integration, Dr. Oakerson argues that it is more productive to view urban areas as local public economies.

There are at least four compelling reasons why, as a country, we must take a new look at how we govern our local communities:

First, since the early 1970s increasing amounts of systematic evidence from diverse sources demonstrates that most reformers' factual descriptions of metropolitan areas are *not* substantiated by evidence, and that many of their recommendations could lead to suboptimal results. For example, economies-of-scale studies show that larger units of government generally realize diseconomies of scale, while smaller units—through a number of means—generally develop arrangements to realize economies of scale.

Second, both the weakening of civil society and the desires of citizens to have greater control over the institutions that affect their lives require that we understand existing conditions and apply our knowledge to rebuilding vital local governing institutions. It is likely that consolidation would further weaken citizen interest and participation.

Third, we need to know how dynamic local public economies function—how the complex interactions between the public, private, and nonprofit sectors work to create political, social, and economic wealth. The reform tradition provides no understanding of these local public economies. Blinded by its normative theory, it sees chaos, and condemns local public economies as fragmented.

Finally, if communities of citizens are "to reflect and choose good government," as Alexander Hamilton characterized the American Experiment in *Federalist* 1,they absolutely must have viable alternatives from which to choose. This book provides at least one such alternative.

I have had an active role in the development of this book. The text originally appeared as *The Organization of Local Public Economies*, a report of the bipartisan U.S. Advisory Commission on Intergovernmental Relations, of which I was appointed chairman in 1982. The mission of this twenty-six-member commission of senators, congressmen, state governors and legislators, and local officials was to provide the country with studies that would improve the governance and performance of the federal system.

From its founding in 1960 the U.S. Advisory Commission championed the reform tradition of local government, and saw fragmentation as the cause of a whole host of problems: diseconomies of scale, operating inefficiencies, lack of systematic regional planning, and unresponsive government. In the mid-'80s, the Commission's position changed.

In 1985 the Commission hired Ronald Oakerson as a senior analyst of governance issues in the federal system. In the same year, the Commission authorized staff to undertake a thorough study of urban governance issues facing citizens and local officials, and selected Dr. Oakerson to head the study. At the full Commission meeting in San Francisco in June 1987, the staff presented *The Organization of Local Public Economies*, its final report and recommendations. This report—subject to professional review by outside academics, practitioners, and elected officials—evaluated existing evidence on the most rational ways to organize governance and provision of services in our urban areas. The report held that no one organizational model could possibly deal efficiently or effectively with the complex dynamics of urban areas. Communities of interest formed around issues that crossed jurisdictional boundaries many times, and many different organizational scales were needed in order to realize economies of scale and foster self-governance.

The report was approved unanimously by the Commission, overturning long-standing recommendations of consolidation of metropolitan areas and abolition of special districts. The Commission now recommended that regional solutions should be built on existing political arrangements, and suggested that special districts could be used effectively by communities to provide services.

I left the Commission in 1992. Two years later, Congress in its "infinite wisdom" saw fit to defund it. This revocation of support followed a long-established trend, revealing in part that both sides of the political fence lacked the conviction and interest to pursue how a dynamic federal system might operate with strong states and local governments.

Dr. Oakerson has brought the original ACIR study up-to-date and has made significant additions. The new title attests to the importance of governance to the creation of the civic metropolis. Governance comes before service provision—along with rebuilding a dynamic citizenship, ensuring a strong citizen role in governance is absolutely necessary to repairing the tattered civic fabric of our metropolitan communities.

It is my hope that this powerful book will stimulate increased reflection and debate about how we ought to govern our lives through local governing institutions. In the face of mounting evidence casting serious doubts on the viability of the "one best" solution, reformers have simply redoubled their efforts. But reform without substantiation is worse than no reform at all: it prevents citizens and communities from contemplating real alternatives, and stunts the growth of a self-governing society. Fostering reflective citizens and communities is far more important to the health of our country than chasing the ghosts of decreasing unit costs through large-scale organizations.

—Robert B. Hawkins, Jr., President
Institute for Contemporary Studies

ACKNOWLEDGMENTS

THE SEEDS OF THIS BOOK were sown during the late '60s and early '70s when I was a graduate student at Indiana University. There I was privileged to study with Vincent Ostrom, who introduced me to what was then—and may still be—a very different way of thinking about metropolitan organization. In 1985 I joined the Advisory Commission on Intergovernmental Relations (ACIR) as a senior analyst, mainly to work on metropolitan issues. At ACIR, Larry Hunter, Dolores Martin, Gary Anderson, John Shannon, John Kincaid, Susannah Calkins, Mark Menchik, Joan Casey, and Debra Dean all contributed to the Commission's rethinking of metropolitan organization. With the strong support of ACIR chairman Robert B. Hawkins, Jr., the Commission directed that we undertake two intensive case studies of highly fragmented metropolitan counties—studies designed to explore the working relationships among local governments and their agencies. Roger B. Parks served as principal investigator for the field studies, which were conducted in the St. Louis and Pittsburgh areas. Others were called upon to give advice and counsel: Louis de Alessi, Robert Bish, James Ferris, Bryan Jones, Ted Kolderie, Daniel Mandelker, Stephen Mehay, Elinor Ostrom, Paul Peterson, Derek Shearer, and Richard Wagner.

In 1987 I wrote a Commission Report titled *The Organization of Local Public Economies*, reviewing the findings of social science research on metropolitan organization and developing a theoretical framework for further study. Gary Anderson and Aaron Bell supplied research assistance. Critical readers of all or portions of the original draft report included Gary M. Anderson, Wayne Anderson, Aaron Bell, Ann Cole, William Colman, Ed Connerly, Larry Hunter, John Kincaid, Susan Lauffer, Michael Libonati,

Dolores Martin, James L. Martin, Richard Moore, Steve Moore, William Niskanen, Vincent Ostrom, Roger Parks, Doug Peterson, Mark Schneider, John Shannon, John Thomas, Gordon Whitaker, Louise White, and Joseph Zimmerman. In the intervening years, the Report has been used as a regular part of the curriculum in the core graduate seminar conducted at the Workshop in Political Theory and Policy Analysis at Indiana University, Bloomington, and I have benefited from numerous comments by Workshop scholars, in particular Elinor Ostrom. In preparing the present volume, I have revised, updated, and elaborated upon the 1987 report. As the rather long recitation of names above indicates, my intellectual debts are many, also including numerous unnamed local officials and citizens interviewed in St. Louis County, Missouri; Allegheny County, Pennsylvania; and DuPage County, Illinois, whose help was essential. Four individuals nonetheless stand out as indispensable contributors to the work presented here: Vincent and Lin Ostrom, whose ideas underlie much of what is found between these covers; Roger Parks, my research colleague and coauthor on numerous occasions, who also provided comments on the revisions incorporated herein; and Bob Hawkins, without whose resolute leadership and support this volume would never have been written, nor revised and published. I also appreciate the daily encouragement of my colleagues at Houghton College and, most of all, the constant support of my wife Elizabeth. I am grateful as well for the editorial assistance of Melissa Stein. Any errors that may remain in these pages are of course my responsibility alone.

1

THE STUDY OF
LOCAL PUBLIC ECONOMIES

INTRODUCTION

THE STUDY OF LOCAL GOVERNMENT in America has long been defined by the sharp edges of its controversies. Despite the introduction of new intellectual approaches and more sophisticated research techniques, the last three decades of the twentieth century have done little to blunt the differences among scholars, in particular over metropolitan issues. Although scholars have made considerable progress in describing and explaining patterns of governance in metropolitan areas, the scholarly community remains sharply divided over issues of reform—how to respond to deep and persistent problems. Often the metropolitan debate seems little more than a sterile exchange of intellectual firepower based on unshakable preconceptions. The intellectual divide is as much philosophical and methodological as it is empirical. The challenge is to find a way of thinking that can be used to build a *more common* understanding of metropolitan problems and possibilities, a way of thinking that unites more than it divides and explains more than it ignores.

Despite progress, deep divisions persist.

On the one hand, new research has led to a new respect for the American tradition of local self-government, rooted in the republicanism of the nation's founders. Rather than simply a vestige of the past, small hometown governments are seen to have an important place in the modern American metropolis, serving as the basic building blocks of metropolitan organization. Moreover, there is a growing recognition that strong local government continues to serve longstanding national purposes, such as representation, community, and civic engagement. In part a rediscovery of

1

nearly forgotten values and principles, the new respect for local institutions is fueled both by historical reflection and by new modes of analysis, much of it associated with the "new institutionalism" in the social sciences.[1]

On the other hand, many if not most scholars and reformers continue to respond to metropolitan problems with a standard set of prescriptions—aggressive annexations, massive consolidations, and sweeping new powers for new metro-wide units of government that would displace as much as possible of the traditional metropolitan order.

For the greater part of the twentieth century the prevailing patterns of local government in America made little sense to most scholars. Mainstream political science and public administration long regarded the American system of local government as a kind of relic—an antique kept for its familiarity and charm but one extremely ill-suited to the demands and prospects of the modern world, especially the modern metropolis. A system created to serve an agrarian republic of scattered rural communities could hardly be expected to meet the needs of an urban and industrial society marked by great concentrations of population. The emergence of metropolitan areas, it was thought, demands the creation of metropolitan governments. Although massive local-government consolidation was long considered the wave of the future, it has never happened, largely because voters for the most part rejected metro-reform proposals at the polls. With the important exception of school districts, the number of local governments in America has continued to grow throughout the century, belying the expectations of reformers who sought precisely the opposite.

Instead of governmental consolidation, the most conspicuous change that came to American local government was the increased use of *contracting*. Rather than producing services through their own departments and bureaus, local governments increasingly entered into contracts with independent producers, who supplied services to the public for a price. The independent producers could be nearby or overlying local governments, or they could be private firms. In fact, some scholars began to argue for privatization—the *private production of public services*—as a preferred alternative in most or even all cases. Much of the ensuing debate over privatization ignored the structure of local government, previously the focus of heated controversy. Perhaps when service production is privatized, local-government structure becomes irrelevant—or at least matters a lot less. This position, however, is not sustainable.

A one-sided focus on *production* ignores the basic function of local government, which is the *provision* of local public services. Provision refers to taxing and spending decisions as distinguished from production and delivery. The distinction is deceptively simple, for provision and production are rarely distinguished in everyday discussions of local government. Yet ability-to-provide and ability-to-produce derive from very different sources. A local government can be an excellent provider of numerous services, yet be unable to produce any of them. Similarly, a local government agency can be an excellent producer of some service even as it leaves provision to other, more appropriate, units of government. Private producers of public services clearly depend on others to make public provision for—to pay for—the services they produce.

The distinction between the provision and production of local public services is critical to a new understanding of local government, one that can make sense of the basic pattern of local government that has developed in America and at the same time lay a foundation for reform. Contracting demonstrates the *possibility* of *separating* provision and production, so that local governments need not produce the entire range of services they provide. The implications, however, extend well beyond contracting. Even though contracting is not always a preferred alternative, the possibility of separating provision and production means that each function can be organized in quite different ways, responsive to distinct criteria. The organization of provision need not be dominated by production-criteria. Ability to produce need not define the viability of a provision unit, any more than ability to provide defines the viability of a production unit. In particular, relatively small provision units can still enjoy the benefits of large scale for the production of specific services.

Viewed through this conceptual lens, metropolitan areas are served by *local public economies* composed of a variety of provision units and production units, both public and private. Local governments for the most part constitute the *provision side* of the local public economy, while a variety of public agencies and private firms compose the *production side*. Each side can be organized on the basis of disparate criteria, then linked in ways that include, but are not limited to, contracting. The search for more responsive provision and more efficient production often leads to the creation of new provision units—new units of government—and new production units—new agencies and firms. As local public economies develop, the number of providers and producers grows, driving up the number of local governments nationwide. The complexity of each local public economy increases as provision and production responsibilities are distributed among a wider variety of independent jurisdictions and organizations. The result is typically a mix of small and large jurisdictions on the provision side alongside a mix of small and large agencies, both public and private, on the production side. From this perspective, the most anomalous feature of American local government—the deviant case—is not the persistence of large numbers of relatively small municipalities, even in metropolitan areas, but the presence of large central-city governments that tend to monopolize a wide range of provision and production responsibilities. Local public economies dominated by monopoly governments can be expected to yield higher tax-prices for local public goods and lower citizen satisfaction with service provision.

Local public economies are the subject of this book. Focused on metropolitan areas in the U.S., the discussion is concerned primarily with the *way of thinking* or mode of analysis needed to understand the basic patterns of metropolitan organization and governance in America revealed by social-science research. Although the methodology employed here uses the same choice-based reasoning typical of microeconomics, it is applied to an institutional arrangement that is neither market nor hierarchy. A *public economy* is not a private economy: use of this concept implies something more than a market metaphor. The basic provision units in a local public economy are *public households*, predominantly local governments but sometimes privately organized associations of homeowners. In either case, creating, organizing, and maintaining a public household is quite a different process from setting up and managing the private household that is a basic unit of market organization. Public households can also be established at various scales of organization—organizing communities of various sizes— and can be created for more or less specialized purposes. Because of their larger scale, public households frequently organize their own production units and control them through administrative hierarchies. In principle, however, any public household can obtain production by contracting-out, either with another public household or with a private firm. Contracts are economic exchanges, but these particular exchanges occur in a political context, where at least one and perhaps both of the parties are likely to be governmental bodies held accountable to their immediate constituents by political means. Moreover, the rules used to govern relationships in a public economy are also a product of political choice, frequently choices made by state legislatures. The governance of a local public economy is necessarily a political task carried out by political means.

At the same time, local public economies are linked to private economies in a variety of ways, some of which distinguish the local scene from the national political economy. A number of observers have emphasized that local communities are much more exposed to the movement of private firms and individuals across borders, and thus they are more constrained than a national community by the effects of economic competition, whether distant or close at hand.[2] The growing globalization of commerce, however, is rapidly transforming even national governments into "local" communities, sharply constrained by international competition.

Despite such constraints, local governments do pursue a range of policies, designed either to facilitate or in some cases to limit local economic development, shaping it to the public demands of their communities. Much of the revenue of local government is raised from commercial and industrial sources that seek to pass their costs on to consumers, most of whom are not local residents. This component of local revenues, however, is also the component most likely to be constrained by economic competition, whether from within the metropolis or from around the world.

Economic development is strongly associated with an expanding set of consumer choices; consumer choice, in turn, creates consumer power vis-à-vis producers. Similarly, viewing local public citizens as analogous to private consumers, a developing public economy is associated with an expanding set of citizen choices among provision possibilities. Neither private nor public economic development is spurred by the provision of standardized goods and services in standardized ways. Rather, the key to development is variety. In a public economy, citizen choice—including both individual and collective choices—creates citizen power vis-à-vis government. Both private producers and governments are potential monopolists. In both cases, monopoly power undermines the power of citizen-consumers to direct economic activity to the satisfaction of their interests. Measured by the interests of citizen-consumers, monopoly power diminishes economic welfare. In a local public economy, citizen satisfaction derives from much the same source as in the private sector—the power of citizen-consumers to make choices, not only among a variety of public goods and services, but also among a range of provision and production arrangements.

While the study of private economies can treat each household as a single consumer, the study of public economies must treat the members of public households as individuals who have independent standing as *citizens*—persons able to participate in multiple, overlapping communities while retaining the same fundamental rights and liberties. The basic units of analysis in a public economy are citizens as members of communities, not local governments as all-purpose suppliers, nor private households as ever-mobile consumers. Citizens are not only consumers but also the governors of local public economies. Citizens participate in governance not only by electing local officials but also by approving or rejecting jurisdictional changes—boundary adjustments and consolidations, incorporations and dissolutions—through popular referenda. The productivity of local public economies may depend on a strong and committed sense of citizenship, as opposed to a narrow sense of "consumership" that eschews local commitments in order to maximize individual mobility. Alexis de Tocqueville, whose *Democracy in America* is widely regarded as the classic expression of the values of American local governance, focused much of his attention on the relationship between citizen engagement and community productivity, observing that citizen engagement led to better roads, better schools, and better law enforcement.[3] Tocqueville's discussion continues to have much relevance today.[4]

It is imperative to recognize that all is not well in metropolitan America today—that there are persistent problems that continue to get worse. From inner-city crime and disorder to suburban sprawl that consumes increasingly scarce open space and adds to transportation difficulties, problems abound. The need for reinvestment in basic physical infrastructure, located both in aging urban neighborhoods and in older suburbs, poses puzzles for the organization of local public economies. There is clearly a need for reform. More precisely, there are problems, in the plural, that demand reforms, also plural. The key to effective reform is a diagnostic capability that supports the crafting of institutional solutions to fit specific problems in context, not wholesale reform designed to fix all problems at once. Metropolitan organization must serve multiple values and purposes; this means that it cannot respond to one problem to the exclusion of others and serve its citizens well. Perhaps citizens intuitively know this simple truth, for all of the related problems of the metropolis are ultimately theirs. Perhaps informed citizenship is the most secure path to reform. If so, the central challenge of American local government today is how to maintain or, in some places, recreate the productivity of local citizen engagement.

Although the focus of this book is on a methodology or way of thinking, it is one that self-consciously adopts a citizen perspective and seeks to examine problems from that perspective. The study of local government in America requires a mode of analysis that *does not foreclose* the possibility that citizens might rationally create multiple local governments and use those governments as the building blocks of a complex local public economy. At the same time, it must also be open to empirical test, seeking to learn from experience and inquiry how best to serve the aggregate, long-term interests of citizens. If the effort is successful, this is a mode of analysis that can be used to explain the choices that citizens make along an institutional path, as they utilize the constraints and opportunities created by previous choices to solve problems and pursue aspirations. It can also be used to diagnose problems and illuminate new choices, clarifying alternatives and estimating their probable consequences. For these purposes, however, warm feelings about citizens and communities will not be enough. The future of American local government depends on the development of a citizen-friendly methodology for its study—and for its reform—that is systematic, rigorous, and empirical. The discussion that follows is strongly focused on these requirements.

DISTINGUISHING PROVISION AND PRODUCTION

Richard A. Musgrave, a public-finance economist, advanced the basic distinction between provision and production as early as 1959: "Provision for public wants . . . does not require public production management, just as public production management does not require provision for public wants. Quite different criteria apply in determining the proper scope of each."[5] In 1961, Vincent Ostrom, a political scientist, joined with Charles M. Tiebout, an economist, and Robert Warren, a political scientist, to recognize the importance of this distinction in the organization of metropolitan areas:

> The separation of the provision of public goods and services from their production opens up the greatest possibility of redefining economic functions in a public service economy. Public control can be maintained in relation to performance criteria in the provision of services, while allowing an increasing amount of competition to develop among the agencies that produce them.[6]

The distinction was slow to affect the ways in which scholars and practitioners think about the functions of local governments. Instead, thinking was long dominated by the idea that "strong" local government requires relatively large general-purpose governments able to *provide and produce* a wide range of goods and services. Production criteria often were dominant in evaluations of local government organization. Discussions of local government "capacity," for example, usually meant capacity to produce. From this perspective, a local government that contracts out *all* of its service production is an inactive, nonperforming government.

The concept of a local public economy distinguishes a provision side from a production side and anticipates that each side will engage in distinctive activities.[7] Provision, in general, refers to collective choices that decide:

- what goods and services to provide (and what are to remain private);
- what private activities to regulate, and the type and degree of regulation to use;
- the amount of revenue to raise, and how to raise it (whether by various forms of taxation or by user pricing);
- the quantities and quality-standards of goods and services to be provided; and
- how to *arrange for* the production of goods and services, linking provision to production.

The basic choice on the provision side is whether to make any sort of provision at all. If no unit of government makes public provision, then provision of the good or service remains a private decision. Many local governments, for example, provide elaborate programs of recreation, while other communities choose to leave the provision of recreation in the private sector. If public provision is undertaken, how to provide services is another basic choice. The two major alternatives are (1) taxing and spending to provide a public good or service or (2) regulating private activity in order to shape private decisions to a public purpose. Provision activities thus include, on the one hand, setting both tax rates and user charges and choosing how to spend public money, and, on the other hand, enacting and enforcing laws or rules that limit private behavior according to public criteria. Finally, if goods and services are to be provided, there follows a basic choice of how to arrange for production—whether by organizing a production unit "in-house" or by selecting and hiring outside producers (public or private). Having arranged for production, provision then requires monitoring the quality and quantity of goods and services produced, representing the interests of citizen-consumers to producers, and holding producers accountable for their performance.[8]

Production, as distinguished from provision, refers to the more technical process of transforming resource inputs into valued outputs—making a product or rendering a service. Part of the task of provision is to establish a link with producers but not necessarily to organize production. In this sense, a provision unit is like a household. One of the basic household decisions, in economic terms, is to decide whether (1) to produce for oneself or (2) to enter the marketplace and purchase a particular good or service. All households produce some goods and services for themselves, whether they include meals, laundry, or a self-built home. The same is true for most public provision units. Modern households tend to be formed more on the basis of provision criteria, such as compatible preferences, than on production criteria, such as skill in housekeeping, meal preparation, and general home repair. Households that lack access to a well-developed market economy, as in many less developed countries, are quite different. Even when service production is delegated to agents (public or private), it is frequently better viewed as "coproduction," a process whereby both a specialized producer (e.g., a teacher) interacts with a citizen-consumer (e.g., a student) to "produce" a good (e.g., education).[9] In this sense, the members of a provision unit, like the members of a household, may still be intimately involved in a production process that relies upon "outside" producers.

A local public economy consists of an array of provision units and production units linked in various ways. The provision units are communities organized to make collective decisions. Governmental arrangements are one way to organize provision units, but there are alternatives as well, chiefly some sort of homeowners association, such as a condominium, organized sub-division, or other sort of Residential Community Association (RCA).[10] Municipalities, townships, counties, school districts, and other special districts may all function as provision units on behalf of various communities, some of which overlap others. Production units are either private firms or public agencies and departments organized by a provision unit (or jointly by two or more provision units). The types of relationships formed among this array of provision and production units are the subjects of chapters 2, 3, and 4.

The distinction between provision and production lays the conceptual foundation for a new approach to organizing local governments and ordering their relationships. As Royce Hanson wrote in 1987, "There is a growing consensus that government has a responsibility to *provide* services and facilities through policies it makes, but services and facilities may be *produced* by either sector, based on values of cost-effectiveness and equity."[11] The primary work of local government increasingly is viewed as providing rather than producing. Different criteria apply to the choice of an organization to *provide* a service than to the choice of an organization to *produce* a service. A local public economy should therefore develop a different mix of organizations on the provision side and on the production side, as it links provision and production in a variety of ways. Organizing the provision side presents very different issues from organizing the production side. Both are equally important, however, in the performance of a local public economy.

THE LOGIC OF PROVISION

The organization of the provision side of a local public economy encounters problems that fall into three main classes: (1) preference revelation, (2) fiscal equivalence, and (3) accountability. Each class of problems suggests criteria for assessing the efficiency of the provision side—criteria quite different from those used to assess production-side efficiency.

Preference Revelation

The problem of individual preference revelation derives from the incentives of individuals to conceal their true preferences for public goods and services if provision is organized on a purely voluntary basis. If provision is voluntary and individuals benefit whether or not they contribute to provision, then the prevailing incentive is to wait for others to contribute. The end-result is either nonprovision or suboptimal provision. Institutionally, what is required is a process of *collective choice*, an arrangement from which individuals cannot simply opt out. Individuals can of course move out of a local jurisdiction, but this is different from opting out of provision while continuing to live in the jurisdiction. The collective-choice requirement can be satisfied in a variety of ways—municipalities, counties, townships, and special districts, as well as private homeowners associations, all provide various institutional capabilities for citizens to act collectively. Citizens make choices and thus reveal preferences within such collective-choice arrangements, but equally important, they can also choose among alternative collective-choice arrangements, not only by moving but also by creating and discarding the local jurisdictions used to structure their collective choices.

Collective choice means that one decision is made for a group composed of individuals with their own preferences. Almost inevitably, collective choices imperfectly reflect individual preferences. The potential for collective distortion of individual preferences is considerable. As John Stuart Mill stated the problem in his essay *On Liberty*, what we call self-government is "not the government of each by himself, but the government of each by all the rest." Majority rule can always be used to produce a collective choice no matter how different individual preferences are. The outcome of this process can be arbitrary and unfair.[12] One way to reduce preference distortion is to rely on multiple units of government as separate provision units.

No particular scale of organization is implied for any single provision unit as long as those individuals immediately affected by provision (or non-provision) are included within its boundaries. The necessary extent of those boundaries varies with the type of good or service in question. The "best" boundaries are those which, minimally, include the affected group of people and, at the same time, are not so large as to include groups of individuals with highly divergent preferences. Other things being equal, the larger the group, the more likely that a large number of members will be dissatisfied with the "average" service level chosen by a majority.[13] In general, a provision unit should define a *community of interest* among a group of people who share some contiguous part of the local geography.

Different goods and services, however, implicate somewhat different communities. The geographic meaning of "local" varies from one problem to another. "Local problems" come in various sizes and shapes, meaning that the minimum-size jurisdiction (one that includes all those immediately affected by provision) varies from one good or service to another. One way to resolve the difficulty is to establish boundaries that embrace the widest set of local problems. Traditional prescriptions for "metropolitan government" attempt to follow this approach. The trouble is that a single large provision unit is then created, one that must act on behalf of a heterogeneous collection of smaller communities with distinct interests. An alternative approach is to rely upon *overlapping* provision units that allow different communities of interest—some small, some large—to be organized simultaneously in relation to different public problems. This creates a set of local governments that Robert A. Dahl likens to "Chinese Boxes," smaller units nested inside larger units.[14]

The criterion of preference revelation requires that individuals affected by common problems, people who perhaps want to provide themselves with collective goods and services, must be able to act collectively. Moreover, the difficulties of collective choice suggest that the power to act collectively, rather than being concentrated in a single jurisdiction, ought to be distributed among diverse communities of interest, some of which are more inclusive than others. The basic task of local governance is then to distribute the powers of collective choice among various, overlapping communities of interest, allowing citizens to associate with a variety of provision units.

Fiscal Equivalence

Efficiency on the provision side of a local public economy varies with the degree of "fiscal equivalence"[15] that is attained by establishing boundaries. This criterion means simply that individuals (households or firms) and groups (neighborhoods or communities) get what they pay for and pay for what they get. Assuming reasonably equal ability to pay, lack of fiscal equivalence is inequitable. Moreover, individuals are given incentives to distort their political expression of "demand" for local public goods, either by inflating their demands if others are required to pay or by depressing their demands if they have to pay more than their share. This undermines the community of interest within a provision unit, creating incentives for individuals to try to improve their own lot at the expense of others rather than by joining with others to improve the welfare of the community.

For some goods and services—those subject to exclusion at the point of consumption—user charges can be utilized to generate fiscal equivalence among individuals. For example, a public swimming pool or golf course can charge admission. Benefit-based taxes can also be used to the same end. Property taxes are generally understood as benefit-based.[16] Unlike a user charge, however, a tax is not contingent upon service delivery. The payment of taxes cannot establish fiscal equivalence apart from the delivery of services. A jurisdiction that contains numerous and varied communities of interest, yet raises revenue on a jurisdiction-wide basis, does not automatically distribute services in a way that is proportional to the revenue generated from various communities. In general, the greater the disparity between jurisdictional boundaries and relevant communities of interest, the more problematical fiscal equivalence becomes.

Accountability

Provision units also must deal with the potential for distortion in principal-agent relationships between citizens and officials. All communities need agents who can represent the interests of community members. The problem is that agents can develop their own interests distinct from the interests of those whom they represent. This is especially the case when the "principal" is a community of people who gain common expression in great part through elected officials. Provision units need to be organized in such a way that individual citizens are able to exercise a significant measure of "voice" so that those who function as agents can be held accountable in the conduct of community affairs.

The ease with which citizens can hold officials accountable is related to the size and preference-heterogeneity of a jurisdiction as well as to the number of functions undertaken. Officials in a single small jurisdiction related to a single coherent community of interest can be held accountable by citizens with relative ease. Officials in a large jurisdiction related to multiple communities of interest can be held accountable by citizens only with much greater difficulty. Single-function units exhibit lower within-unit costs of accountability than do multifunction units, although multiplying the number of single-function units can increase the costs of accountability overall. In general, the costs of holding officials accountable to citizens are minimized by provision units that are closely matched to communities of interest.

Transaction Costs as a Limiting Factor

Organizing the provision side of a local public economy is a multidimensional problem involving a range of decisions—boundary choices used to define a community of interest, a choice of taxing instruments and the way those instruments are used in terms of fiscal equivalence, and the creation of opportunities for citizens to hold officials accountable to a community of interest. All three criteria—preference revelation, fiscal equivalence, and accountability—point to the desirability of allowing citizens to create multiple provision units so that each unit is as closely matched as possible to an underlying community of interest. Interests shared on a small scale should be organized by relatively small units; interests shared on a larger scale should be organized with reference to larger, overlapping jurisdictions.

None of the three criteria, however, suggest a *limit* to the number of provision units created.[17] The limiting factor consists of *transaction costs,* the costs involved in organizing and operating such units.[18] The conduct of both private and public business entails transaction costs. In the private sector, transaction costs include the time and effort devoted to such activities as searching for buyers or sellers, bargaining over price, and enforcing contracts. In the public sector, transaction costs consist of the time and effort devoted to making collective decisions, including the cost of elections, communications and meetings, and reporting to secure accountability. Included are the costs of citizen participation in addition to the costs of official action.

To some extent, the values associated with preference revelation, fiscal equivalence, and accountability have to be traded off against the transaction costs associated with creating and then maintaining a separate provision unit. Organizing costs are present mainly at the start of an enterprise, but the marginal costs of operating a separate unit—the additional operating costs of adding a provision unit—are continuing. The *net cost of* adding a unit, however, is not equal to the *total* cost of operation. Presumably, adding a unit relieves other units of part of their work (or precludes work from being added). The net cost of an additional unit is the price of achieving more precise preference revelation, greater fiscal equivalence, and greater (or less costly) accountability.[19]

Choosing an appropriate number of provision units presents an optimizing problem for citizens. Consider, for example, the organization of school districts as separate provision units—separate, that is, from municipal, county, or township governments organized to provide a range of community services. Electing a board of education separate from a city council entails some obvious additional costs—elections, personnel, and meetings—mostly transaction costs. If the same community is organized by both a school district and, perhaps, a municipality, then fiscal equivalence is not an issue. The difference must lie in the areas of preference expression and accountability. By electing a school board separately, preferences about schools do not have to be expressed simultaneously with preferences about police protection or garbage collection as voters make electoral choices. Accountability for the performance of schools can be separated from accountability for the performance of other functions. Separate accountability for schools is presumably worth the net cost of a separate provision unit. Keeping schools "out of politics" means keeping educational issues from being confounded with other issues in a community.

By contrast, a community may find that police protection and garbage collection do not warrant separate provision units within the same community. Although these two functions are quite distinct, as long as the same community is involved, it may be possible to economize on transaction costs by combining provision for both services in a single unit.

The number of provision units may also change over time, when, for example, citizens decide to create a new municipality within an existing county jurisdiction. The question in this case is whether a community finds that its interests and preferences have become sufficiently different from others in the county to justify the creation of a new provision unit. The initial costs of creating a new municipal jurisdiction are substantial, usually including at least the costs of petitioning and voting. The net operating costs are also apt to be positive, adding a new mayor and council to the existing county provisioning apparatus, although the work load of a county council and other elected county officials would decrease somewhat. The potential benefits lie in the areas of preference revelation, fiscal equivalence, and accountability. More precise preference revelation may enable citizens in the new municipality to obtain a substantially different level and mix of services. Greater fiscal equivalence may lead to a more efficient allocation of resources among competing services and communities, considered from a countywide perspective. Accountability secured with respect to a more compact community may enable citizens to obtain a closer match between their preferences and local government performance. Citizen-participation costs entailed in obtaining accountability may actually decrease, owing to the greater accessibility of officials. The question that local citizens have to decide is whether these advantages outweigh the total organizing costs and net operating costs of creating and maintaining a new provision unit.

The consolidation of existing provision units poses the same question in reverse. Are the net gains from eliminating a provision unit greater than the costs calculated in terms of preference revelation, fiscal equivalence, and accountability? Communities must also sometimes consider a potential redistribution factor. Less wealthy communities may gain from associating with more wealthy communities in a single provision unit, a calculation that must be discounted to some extent by political risk. This factor then has to be added to the net gain calculated in terms of operating costs.

Because organizing and operating provision units are costly activities, one can expect diminishing returns as preference revelation, fiscal equivalence, and accountability are improved. Perfection on any of these criteria is out of reach. Citizens (or their representatives) must decide whether increased performance with respect to the major provision criteria is worth the added cost of organizing and operating one more provision unit. At some point, as the number of provision units per citizen increases, it becomes more efficient to assign new functions to existing units rather than create new units to organize provision. Part of the rationale for multipurpose units is to economize on transaction costs. This does not mean, however, that multipurpose units are always preferred to special-purpose units. The answer varies from case to case.

The efficiency of the provision side of a local public economy depends upon a complex set of calculations and trade-offs, some of which are inherently subjective and all subject to change over time. There is no way of determining provision-side efficiency apart from the choices that citizens make. Reformers have often focused a great deal of concern on the "proliferation" of units of local government. On this basis, rules have been proposed, and to some extent enacted, that tend to limit the ability of citizens to create new units.[20] Even in the absence of such rules, however, it should not be assumed that units proliferate without limit. There is no reason to presume that citizens are unable to take into account the costs as well as the benefits of creating an additional unit, even if neither side of the trade-off can be quantified with precision. Moreover, some communities resist incorporation, and others choose to dissolve or to merge with neighboring communities.[21] Growth in the number of units in a local public economy does not imply that growth is unconstrained.

THE LOGIC OF PRODUCTION

Organization on the production side, in contrast to provision, is based upon considerations having to do with the technical transformation of resource "inputs" into product or service "outputs." Unfortunately, no one has been able to demonstrate a "recipe"[22] for the production of good policing or good education, although somewhat more is known about producing good streets and good refuse collection. Almost all local public goods and services, however, depend upon the availability of specific time-and-place information, such as neighborhood conditions, to support effective production choices.[23] This suggests that the scale and organization of the production process should allow producers to make locally informed judgments. These considerations are much different from those involved in the organization of an "assembly line."

Coproduction

Traditionally, production-side considerations have placed a heavy emphasis on the importance of "management," namely, the coordination of human and material resources. Human resources are generally obtained through an employer-employee relationship. Many public services also depend, however, on the productive efforts of citizen-consumers as an integral part of the production process. The participation of citizen-consumers in production, as distinguished from provision, is called "coproduction."[24] Unlike employees, citizens are not as easily subject to the direction of a professional manager. While it is well known that the productivity of local public agencies, such as schools and police departments, frequently depends on the cooperation of cit-izens, it is not well understood how to incorporate citizens into a production process. Yet citizen-consumers are often a crucial source of time-and-place information. The need for coproduction must be joined with traditional con-cerns for professional management when organizing the production side of a local public economy. The willingness of citizens to contribute to the pro-duction side is often a crucial factor in the ability of a production unit to address relevant community needs and preferences.

Economies of Scale

An important distinction exists between local public *goods*, which tend to be capital intensive, and local public *services*, which tend to be labor intensive. Capital intensive goods, such as water and sewer systems, are more likely to be characterized by "economies of scale," namely, a decrease in the average per-unit cost of production as the scale of production increases.[25] Labor-intensive services, such as police protection and education, are more likely to exhaust potential economies of scale quickly, in part because of the greater dependence of human services on specific time-and-place information. Different goods and services are apt to be characterized by different economies of scale—some may be very small, others quite large. This logic also extends to different service components. Much different economies may also be involved in increasing the level of production per capita for a given population as opposed to extend-ing the same level of production per capita to a larger population.

When economies of scale happen to be closely matched to the scale of organization of a provision unit, in-house production is feasible. A small municipality, for example, can efficiently produce police patrol services; important economies of scale can be captured up to about four to five offi-cers, after which further expansion entails constant (and eventually decreasing) returns to scale.[26] Similarly, a large municipality can efficiently undertake in-house production of the more capital-intensive components of services, such as a police crime-lab. Frequently, however, provision-side criteria lead to the establishment of provision units, both small and large, that are not well matched to economies of scale for particular services and service-components. This is the circumstance that most often leads to the *separate organization* of production.

Coordination Costs as a Limiting Factor

The production and delivery of goods and services can be broken down into a large number of components, distinguishing direct-service components delivered to citizens from various support-service components delivered to direct service producers. Each component may be associated with a different economy of scale (although services typically exhibit constant returns over a broad range). Yet the different components of service production require coordination to varying degrees. Coordination is costly, mainly in terms of the time and effort devoted to transactions. The transaction costs associated with coordination can be expected to limit the proliferation of separate production units much as transaction costs limit the proliferation of separate provision units. Organizing an additional unit to capture economies of scale in the production of a particular service component also creates coordination costs between different units. An optimal number of production units depends on a trade-off between scale economies, on the one hand, and coordination economies, on the other. Coordination costs also arise, however, *within* production units. The relevant consideration therefore is the *net* coordination cost of adding a production unit, not the *total* cost of coordination.[27]

LINKING PROVISION TO PRODUCTION

Distinguishing the provision side from the production side of a local public economy opens up a range of possibilities for *linking* a provision unit to production units. The main options are as follows:

- *In-house production.* A provision unit organizes its own production unit. This is the traditional model of local organization. Municipalities organize municipal departments for police, fire, public works, and so forth.
- *Coordinated production.* Two or more production units (organized by their respective provision units) coordinate their production activities, in whole or in part. Two police departments, for example, may cooperate to investigate a string of burglaries affecting both jurisdictions.
- *Joint production.* Two or more provision units jointly organize a single production unit. A number of small municipalities, for example, may jointly finance and administer a dispatch center for their police and fire departments.
- *Intergovernmental contracting.* A provision unit contracts for production with another provision unit, which assumes responsibility for organizing production.
- *Private contracting.* A provision unit contracts with a private vendor, who is responsible for organizing a production unit.
- *Franchising.* A provision unit sets production standards and selects a private producer, but allows individual citizen-consumers to choose whether to

purchase the service. For example, a municipality, instead of providing trash collection, may grant a franchise to a private collector who is then authorized exclusively to sell the service to residents in that jurisdiction.

- *Vouchering.* A provision unit sets production standards and decides on the level of provision (through its taxing and spending powers), but allows individuals (or groups) to engage different producers, public or private, at their discretion. Vouchers, distributed to individuals by government, are now most frequently used in housing and social services, and combine public finance of services with individual choice of service suppliers.

Public administration theory long assumed that the best sort of local government was a "full-service" government—analogous to a vertically integrated business firm—performing both provision and production functions for a full range of local public goods and services. On the provision side, it was assumed that a relatively large general-purpose government is best able to balance the demands of competing concerns and interests within a single budget document. On the production side, it was assumed that coordination and economies of scale are best achieved when a single local-government manager is able to assign functions among subordinate units. Both assumptions overlook the advantages of greater variety in organization.

The potential variety in organizing both the provision side and the production side, and in relating provision to production, is much greater than ordinarily assumed. More and more local governments have begun to see their primary role as one of "provisioning" as distinct from producing, choosing to produce only when in-house production, through a government bureau or department, is the best alternative available. The ability to separate provision from production also frees the provision side of a local public economy from production constraints, allowing it to be organized on the basis of provision criteria, subject only to the limitation inherent in the costs of organizing and operating additional provision units.

METROPOLITAN GOVERNANCE

The governance of a local public economy characterized by multiple provision and production units is not likely to be vested in any single provision unit within the local arena. Governance is neither provision nor production. Instead, governance requires the ability to make and enforce *rules* for organizing the local public economy, establishing an institutional framework within which patterns of provision and production emerge from the choices of local citizens and officials. The governance process includes the *resolution of conflict* among participants, as well as the maintenance of agreeable and equitable arrangements. The work of governance is separable from both provision and production.

The basic task of governing a local public economy is to put together, and periodically adjust, a set of rules that enables citizens and their local officials to seek out and create mutually beneficial provision and production arrangements. The relevant rules pertain to (1) organization on the provision side (which depends upon collective choice capabilities, tax instruments, the use of "police" powers in regulation, elections and referenda, and the public accountability of officials); (2) the organization of public production; and (3) relationships between provision units and production units (especially contracting and joint production).

When conflict occurs (as for example over municipal boundaries or tax incidence), governance arrangements must exist to apply general rules to specific cases and to encourage participants to reach settlements. If settlements cannot be reached on the basis of existing rules, new rules may be needed. Fiscal disparities among provision units are a potential source of conflict in most highly differentiated local public economies. Adjustments in the fiscal rules governing revenue capabilities—in particular the availability, and possible sharing, of various tax bases—are often responses to fiscal conflict. The highly differentiated local public economies usually found in metropolitan areas do require a form of metropolitan governance, but it is a form of governance that depends on citizens to make the basic structural choices within a framework of rules.

The "organization" of a local public economy can therefore be understood at two levels. One is the *governance level*—the maintenance of rules, including rule-prescribing, rule-applying, and rule-enforcing facilities, which establish a framework within which provision and production arrangements emerge. The other is the *provision/production level*—the maintenance of specific provision and production arrangements with respect to specific goods and services in specific communities of interest. Both levels of organization can be distinguished from *performance*—the patterns of goods and services actually provided, produced, and received.[28]

Some of the most controversial empirical questions about local government—especially in metropolitan areas—are those that concern linkages between levels of organization and between organization and performance. Does jurisdictional fragmentation, allowed by permissive incorporation rules, result in uncoordinated service delivery? Do overlapping jurisdictions, created by allowing citizens to form special districts in addition to municipalities, engender duplication of effort and a misallocation of resources? Or does the greater variety of organization at the provision/production level, generated by a governance level that allows citizens to create multiple provision units, lead to greater efficiency and responsiveness with respect to a broad range of local services?

EQUITY

The governance of a local public economy also includes reference to efforts to maintain some level of distributional equity among citizens. Two basic approaches have been followed in dealing with this issue. One approach is to enlarge the boundaries of provision units so as to include a heterogeneous community with respect to income. Pooling revenues over this heterogeneous community while distributing services according to need would generate equity. Public resources could be closely matched to public needs. An alternative approach is to rely upon overlapping provision units to pool revenue on a larger scale and redistribute resources to provision units considered to be disadvantaged according to a set of criteria. Both approaches have been followed to some degree in the United States. School district consolidation is perhaps the major example of the former approach, but local district consolidation has been accompanied by further efforts to redistribute resources on a statewide basis in many states, utilizing complex formulas to divide state funds among local school districts. An intermediate approach has been pioneered in the Minneapolis–St. Paul area, where revenues from commercial and industrial property are partially shared on a metropolitan-wide basis.

Any effort to redistribute resources represents a departure from the criterion of fiscal equivalence. Arranging the boundaries of provision units to encompass a deliberately heterogeneous community is inconsistent with fiscal equivalence. "Getting what you pay for and paying for what you get" is also a principle of equity, albeit not redistributional equity. Relying on redistribution by overlapping jurisdictions combines the principle of fiscal equivalence as a first-order criterion of organization with redistributional equity as a second-order criterion. Efforts to redistribute then operate only as the first-order criteria generate patterns of provision that lie outside acceptable limits of resource distribution. A critical question, one that can only be answered by empirical research, is whether the use of the first-order criteria to generate a highly differentiated pattern of organization *creates* serious problems of equity, which then have to be addressed by overlapping units. In more traditional language, the question is this: Does fragmentation cause inequity?

CIVIL SOCIETY

Generations of scholars have been largely unable to conceive of metropolitan governance without metropolitan government. Metropolitan *integration* was, in this view, foreclosed by governmental *fragmentation*. This is a one-sided focus on government, however, that neglects the role of civil society—the realm of voluntary association—in the process of governance. The absence of a metropolitan government does not necessarily preclude the creation of a metropolitan civil society. Complex local public economies tend to develop numerous voluntary associations of local governments and officials, plus citizen associations, that transcend local boundaries. Moreover, it is clear that highly fragmented metro areas depend on civic involvement at every level. Small municipalities depend heavily on either volunteers or part-timers to serve as public officials. Even professional associations depend on civic-minded police chiefs or fire chiefs. The study of metropolitan areas plainly must include the role played by civil society, in particular, its role in metropolitan integration.

CONCLUSION

Distinguishing provision and production has broad implications for the organization and governance of a local public economy.[29] Consider the following inferences:

- Both private and intergovernmental contracting are viable alternatives to in-house production.
- Very small local governments are potentially viable as "pure provision" units.
- An optimal mix of provision units in a local public economy is likely to range in size from large to small, with some units overlapping others.
- An optimal set of production arrangements is apt to mix in-house production with contracting out for different "components" of the same service.
- An optimal pattern of organization can emerge among provision and production units without being planned by any single set of decision-makers.
- Metropolitan governance is possible without metropolitan government.
- Equity may be better served by redistributing resources through overlapping jurisdictions than by adjusting local boundaries.
- Civil society in the metropolis is strengthened, not weakened, by governmental fragmentation.

These implications, among others, are explored in the chapters that follow, in the course of analyzing provision and production problems and arraying evidence on key questions. Chapter 2 takes up the most obvious implication of distinguishing provision and production—that each function can be separately organized and then linked through contracting. If provision and production can be separately organized, it follows that different criteria can be used in organizing the provision side and the production side of a local public economy, the subjects of chapter 3 and chapter 4 respectively. Chapter 3 considers issues of jurisdictional type and size, and chapter 4 employs an industrial organization model to explain prevailing patterns of public service production and delivery in metro areas. Both provision and production decisions are made within a set of rules common to the local public economy, the result of metropolitan governance, discussed in chapter 5. This chapter is concerned not with the governance of separate local governments, but with the governance of the local public economy as a distinct level of organization, highlighting the role of civil society in the process. Chapter 5 also raises issues of equity and considers how to maintain equity in a governmentally fragmented structure. Chapter 6 concludes with a discussion of the civic metropolis, arguing that a civic model is not only required to explain the superior efficiency of highly fragmented metro areas but also needed to fulfill the promise of the American political tradition in local terms.

2

SEPARATING
PROVISION AND PRODUCTION

INTRODUCTION

THE PROVISION AND PRODUCTION of services are conceptually very different activities, suggesting the possibility of separating them in practice—organizing each one independently of the other. The separate organization of provision and production depends, however, on the viability of *contracting* as a method for linking provision to production. Contracting is viable to the extent that provision units are able to choose between an in-house production unit and an external producer *on their merits*, rather than discounting external producers because of the need to contract-out. The viability of contracting does not require that contracting-out is inherently superior to producing in-house, only that it is *not* inherently inferior. To the extent that contracting is a viable option for linking provision and production, the potential variety in the organization of local public economies is greatly increased. If, however, contracting-out is inherently inferior to in-house production, the distinction between provision and production becomes much less significant in the organization of a local public economy.

Some local governments do little or no contracting, while others approximate "pure provision" units, organizing hardly any production in-house. What leads provision units to choose one option over the other? A number of factors potentially affect the viability of contracting-out. One is the incentive of provision-side officials to choose the contract option. To the extent that contracting is not incentive-compatible on the provision side, its relevance diminishes. Other factors include the ability of provision units to monitor the performance of independent producers, to compare the performance of one production unit to another, and to change producers as needed. Questions also arise concerning the ability of private producers to make needed capital investments without a guaranteed stream of future revenue. Private producers are often thought to be less appropriate for certain services, e.g., police, but the possibility of intergovernmental contracting tends to obviate this objection. Finally, all forms of specialization and exchange are limited by the "extent of the market." Are most metropolitan areas big enough to generate alternative producers within reach of providers? How much competition is required among producers to make contracting work?

VARIATION IN CONTRACTING-OUT

Contracting, both private and intergovernmental, is widely practiced: nearly all municipalities contract-out for at least one service. Most municipalities, however, limit contracting to only a small proportion of their service responsibilities—suggesting, perhaps, the superiority of in-house production. Although in-house production has remained the norm, the use of contracting nonetheless has become increasingly popular over the last several decades.

Significant change in both the extent and the type of municipal contracting occurred in the 1970s and 1980s. Contracting in the period prior to 1970 was heavily biased toward the public sector. The United States Advisory Commission on Intergovernmental Relations (ACIR) found in its 1972 study of interlocal arrangements that intergovernmental contracting (i.e., contracting with another unit of government to supply a service) was the preferred alternative to in-house municipal production.[1] Perhaps because of a lack of private vendors and/or a lingering concern with corrupt practices in the awarding of contracts, municipal governments avoided private service producers in favor of governmental jurisdictions when shedding service production. The reluctance to use private vendors had diminished significantly by the early 1980s. The proportion of communities reporting at least one private service contract exceeded the percent of cities reporting at least one intergovernmental service contract by 18 percentage points by 1983. This finding reflected the growing number of private service contracts, however, not an absolute decline in intergovernmental contracting.

By the 1980s, municipal contracting was dominated by two quite disparate service categories—public works and health and social welfare services—both concentrated within the private sector. Over half of the municipalities in the sample had contracted with at least one private vendor for these services. Governmental units are the dominant contract producers only for public safety services. Among private producers, for-profit vendors dominate service contracts for general government services, transportation and public works. Their nonprofit counterparts have a significant edge in service contracts for cultural activities (e.g., libraries and museums) and a slight advantage in the proportion of municipalities contracting with them for health and welfare services. Neighborhood associations, while an important new contract producer, to date have had a negligible impact on the level of private service contracting. Their greatest contribution to service production is in the area of public safety and health and welfare.

Empirical studies of garbage collection,[2] electrical power,[3] fire protection,[4] police protection,[5] and an assortment of custodial and general services[6] have found that contracted service production nets significant cost savings over in-house government production. These findings support, but do not fully establish, the viability of contracting as an arrangement for linking provision to production. The presence of cost savings is usually explained in terms of economies of scale in production and the benefits of greater competition on the production side of the local public economy. The viability of contracting also depends, however, on the *quality* of services being produced under contract. The Department of Housing and Urban Development (HUD) explored this question in a series of intensive case studies, which examined eight services in twenty cities, half of which produced services in-house and half of which contracted-out.[7] The research objective was to compare the efficiency of service production while taking account of variation in service quality; the results were mixed. On the one hand, contracting cities exhibited a pronounced tendency toward more efficient service production. On the other hand, efficiency gains from contracting exhibited substantial variation, and some cities producing services in-house were more efficient than contracting cities. Contracting-out, although more often successful than not, was not consistently superior to in-house production. Its viability as an option was nonetheless confirmed in these studies.

The precise advantage or disadvantage of contracting, with respect to specific goods and services, can be expected to vary from one provision unit to another. Contracting is not uniformly preferred to in-house production for any given service type across all provision units in all circumstances. Small communities may choose to contract out for reasons of economies of scale that larger communities can capture in-house; both small and large communities may choose to do so for reasons of competition, but the extent of competition may vary from one local public economy to another. In particular, the organization of the *provision* side of a local public economy has substantial impact on the organization of the *production* side.

EXPLAINING THE DECISION TO CONTRACT-OUT

Table 2.1 summarizes the results of a multivariate analysis of municipal contracting conducted for the ACIR by Dolores T. Martin and Robert M. Stein.[8] The dependent variable is the percentage of municipal functions in which at least one contract is reported. Most of the independent variables included in the model measure some aspect of provision arrangements, or rules governing the organization of the provision side. Several of these variables are significantly related to the use of contracting, as measured here. The model correctly predicted a little more than 84 percent of the cases.

Among rules affecting the provision side, two types are significant: (1) state-imposed property-tax limitations on local government and (2) the relative ease of municipal annexation and consolidation. More stringent property tax limitation and more constraining procedures for municipal annexation and consolidation are both associated with more contracting. (Expenditure limitation is not significant.) One interpretation of these findings is that local public economies that place more power in the hands of citizens—to approve increases in tax rates and adjustments of municipal boundaries—tend to engage in more contracting. Tax burden was not significant in this model, although this finding is not supported by other empirical work.[9]

Another variable that significantly affects the degree of municipal contracting is the number of local governments located within a municipality's Metropolitan Statistical Area (MSA). This variable can be interpreted as a measure of the "extent" of the local government market for services. The number of provision units in a local public economy is equivalent to the number of potential consumers of externally produced services. At least since Adam Smith, economists have hypothesized that specialization in production varies with the extent of a market. The greater the number of consumers in a market, the more specialized production becomes. A greater degree of contracting in a local public economy is associated with greater specialization on the production side. Increasing the number of provision units within a local public economy tends to increase the reliance on contracting of any single provision unit within that setting. Differentiation on the provision side has an amplified effect on the degree of differentiation on the production side.

The relationship of municipal population size to contracting is curvilinear in this model. Both small and large municipalities tend to contract out more than midsize municipalities.[10] Economies of scale may account for the greater propensity of small municipalities to engage in contracting. The same explanation is unavailable, however, to explain greater contracting by

Table 2.1
Logit Estimates for Degree of Municipal Contracting, 1982–83

Variable	Logit Estimate	Standard Error
Intercept	3.72	.723
Population^2	.524–5E*	.160–5E
Population	−.000*	−.000
Number of units of local government in SMSA	.001*	.000
Tax burden	−3.71	.346
Number full-time equivalent public employees	−15.79*	11.03
Property tax limitation (length of time in effect, 0=none)	.182*	.081
Local expenditure limitation (length of time in effect, 0=none)	.103	.082
State centralization	−.039	−.018
Ease of local annexation and consolidation	−.173*	−.055
City manager form	.328*	.124
Percent of work force unionized	.004	.010

−2 Log Likelihood Ratio = 1,561   ×2 of log likelihood ratio = 75.8*
Percent cases predicted = 84.1   Gamma = .308*
Percent of cases incorrectly predicted by categories of dependent variable:
0%–10% of services contracted = 9.7
10%–33% of services contracted = 0
>33% of services contracted = 16.5
* p < .05

large municipalities. Indeed, one rationale for increasing the size of local governments, from a traditional perspective, is to avoid dependence on outside producers—to be self-sufficient. This effect appears to be quite limited. Consistent with an economies-of-scale argument, however, is a diseconomies-of-scale argument. Average costs are generally understood to have a U-shaped relationship to scale of production. As production increases from zero, average costs initially decline, then level off, and finally after a point begin to increase. One important variant of diseconomies of scale in production is diseconomies of scale in management. As the size of a provision unit increases, beyond some point, scale economies attained as a technical matter of production may be offset by management difficulties that multiply as the provision unit attempts to organize more and more production in-house. From this perspective, the tendency toward increased reliance on contracting by larger municipalities reflects an effort by public managers to simplify their internal management problems—by securing outside production of selected service components.

The sample of municipalities used to generate the estimates in table 2.1 was limited to municipalities over 10,000 in population. If smaller provision units were included, the relationship between small size and a greater reliance on contracting would almost certainly be more pronounced. The ACIR field study of a highly differentiated local public economy in St. Louis County, Missouri, examined contracting in three service areas— police, fire, and streets—for ninety municipalities ranging in size from less than 1,000 residents to about 55,000 residents.[11] Municipalities under 10,000—and especially those under 5,000—relied on service contracts with external producers much more heavily than larger municipalities. Indeed, for the production of basic services delivered directly to citizens—police patrol, fire fighting, street repair—municipalities tended to shift to in-house production at the minimum point where significant economies of scale can be captured. For these basic services, the size threshold for in-house production appears to be quite low—somewhere around 1,000 residents for basic street services and 2,000 residents for police patrol.[12]

THE RELEVANCE OF PROVISION ARRANGEMENTS

In order for citizen-consumers to realize a benefit from contracting, there must also exist a provision unit able to acquire information about alternative producers, choose a production mode, select a specific producer, negotiate a contract, and monitor performance. These are not idle tasks. They require agents who bring a citizen-consumer perspective to their work and who remain alert to alternative possibilities. Provision-side activities are crucial to the utility of contracting. Because provision arrangements are public, the treatment of contracting as a form of "privatization" is somewhat misleading. Contracting-out to a private firm privatizes only the production side, not the provision side. Despite evidence that contracting offers substantial efficiency gains, empirical research also discloses considerable variability in those gains. Variation in the performance of activities on the provision side may account for much of the variation in efficiency gains. It is not difficult to imagine situations in which contracting harms, rather than helps, the interests of citizens. The possibilities range from "sweetheart" contracts in which the chosen vendor is not, for one reason or another, the most efficient, to outright corruption of public officials. Corruption, however, is a problem on the provision side. The use of contracting does not relieve citizens and officials of the need to maintain appropriate provision arrangements, including accountability for the expenditure of public funds.

Provision arrangements are also important because provision determines how efficiency gains from contracting will be distributed. Who benefits from contracting? Do citizen-consumers derive a benefit, either from tax savings, increased levels of service, or both? Or do local government politicians, managers, and bureaucrats grab the lion's share of benefit by in effect distributing the efficiency gains from contracting in ways beneficial to their particular interests, especially by increasing provision levels rather than decreasing revenues?

The ACIR study contains some interesting results relevant to these questions. First, there is evidence that efficiency gains from contracting tend to reduce municipal expenditures when municipalities contract out less than 25 percent of their service responsibilities. Second, however, there is evidence that gains from contracting tend *not* to reduce expenditures when contracting moves beyond 25 percent of service responsibilities. The meaning of this finding is unclear. Stein and Martin[13] speculated that bureau managers who contract out some portion of their workload reach a bargain with city managers that allows the gains from contracting to remain within the bureau. The gains then go toward increased service provision rather than decreased spending. Alternatively, the finding may mean that citizens choose to support increased service provision, given the lower tax-price for services made possible by contracting. If there are efficiency gains from contracting, it follows that the more a municipality is able to contract-out (presumably within some limit that varies from place to place), the lower the tax-price of services provided. As the tax-price decreases, the quantities demanded by citizens can be expected to increase.

The fundamental importance of the contracting option is the ability of a provision unit *to choose* the production arrangement. The availability of a marketplace on the production side does not necessarily mean that provision units should always choose to enter the market as collective consumers, rather than produce for themselves.[14] A basic function of provision units is to decide how to arrange for production. For example, a study of municipal contracting in Los Angeles County[15] found that, in general, contracting is associated with lower expenditures; this seems to argue for the superiority of contracting. However, an analysis of municipalities that contract with the Los Angeles County Sheriff for production of police services discovered the following: communities that want a relatively low level of policing seem to do well by contracting, but communities that want a higher level of policing do well producing for themselves. In other words, by contracting, communities that demand less police protection can get what they want without having to organize a police department; however, those communities that demand more police protection would find a contract arrangement with the county sheriff more expensive than in-house production.[16] In situation like this one, it is the ability of provision units to choose how to arrange for production, and not the inherent superiority of one production mode over another, that becomes the key factor in determining efficiency outcomes.

"PURE PROVISION" UNITS

Are Small Local Governments Nonviable?

The issue of local government viability was addressed in some detail by the ACIR in a 1969 report on *State Aid to Local Government*. The Commission urged states to establish criteria of viability to be used to assess the worthiness of a local unit to receive state funds or to compel its dissolution. The relevant criteria were seen to include (1) measures of fiscal capacity, (2) economic diversity, and (3) minimum population and geographic size. The third criterion was assumed to be relevant to realizing economies of scale and making appropriate use of both specialized personnel and new technology. The states were commended for having used their powers over local governance to reduce greatly the number of school districts in the nation and were urged to undertake the same course of action with respect to general-purpose governments.[17]

Although the language of the report presupposed a large number of nonviable units, the ACIR did not propose specific criteria to ascertain their existence until 1981. In its comprehensive report on *State and Local Roles in the Federal System*, the Commission recommended that states use one of two minimum standards of viability: (1) that any local government (general or special-purpose) located in the urbanized portion of a Standard Metropolitan Statistical Area (SMSA) have the equivalent of at least one full-time employee; or (2) that all general-purpose units "perform at least four functions, or only two functions, provided that each of the two constitutes at least 10% of the jurisdiction's current expenditure budget." The Commission further recommended dissolution of local governments that do not meet either of these standards. The major empirical finding cited to support the recommendation consisted of 1977 Census of Governments statistics reporting 4,424 municipalities, 8,673 townships, 17,534 special districts, and 280 school districts with no full-time equivalent employment, as well as 9,614 municipalities with a population under 1,000.[18]

Distinguishing provision and production raised serious questions about the basic logic of this recommendation, and it was repealed by the ACIR in June 1987.[19] Units that "perform" few functions in the sense of both providing and producing goods and services can be quite viable—and active—as provision units. Jurisdictions that produce little or nothing for themselves are nonetheless active in shopping for services from among potential vendors, both public and private, and in raising revenue to pay for those services. These activities, usually undertaken by citizens who serve as part-time officials, give representation to the interests of citizen-consumers in those jurisdictions. Criteria pertaining to the number of full-time equivalent employees are irrelevant to the viability of a provision unit. Criteria pertaining to number of functions "performed" are similarly irrelevant, when performance is defined to include both provision and production.

These conclusions are supported by the ACIR study of St. Louis County,[20] which contained twenty-two municipalities with an estimated population under 1,000 in 1984. Nearly all of these small units were active as providers of the two basic services provided by municipalities in St. Louis County—police and streets. Only a single municipality failed to report provision in both service areas. Missouri law requires that municipalities with a resident population of 400 or more persons provide full-time police services. Among the nine municipalities not required to make provision by state law, only one, with a population of thirty-one persons, failed to make explicit provision for police services beyond that provided by county police. Six contracted to receive service (two of which supplement the contract with their own part-time producers) and two maintained their own part-time departments. Street services indicate somewhat less activity. Four municipalities, including the single nonprovider of police services, reported no expenditures for street services in 1985; their average population was 196 persons. (At this scale of organization, however, there is a distinct possibility of making regular provision for street repair at intervals that exceed one year.) Still, the average level of provision among the remaining municipalities was substantial. The average street expenditure for these eighteen municipalities was about $75 per household, compared to an average street expenditure of $104 per household for the great majority of county municipalities (those for which comparable data were available). Information supplied by ten out these eighteen municipalities disclosed only one that produced any street services in-house. Unlike police, most contracting for street services was with private producers.

The appropriateness of earlier ACIR recommendations, urging states to establish criteria of viability but not proposing anything specific, is more difficult to evaluate. The adaptive capabilities of local public economies require that provision units be subject to modification, including the possibility of both dissolution and merger. The governance processes of local public economies typically contain procedures that allow these changes to occur. The basic question is about process: what decision-makers are best situated to judge the viability of a provision unit? Specifically, can local citizens make these judgments for themselves, or is state intervention needed?

Do "Pure Provision" Units Have Advantages on the Provision Side?

The separation of provision and production casts a much different light on the potential economic viability and usefulness of very small local governments. As is now widely accepted, inability to produce does not entail inability to provide. The potential for contracting out the production of public goods and services (with either public or private vendors) offers the possibility of maintaining "pure provision" units—local governments that produce little or nothing for themselves, but remain very active as providers. The implications extend well beyond the potential viability of small local governments. A number of municipalities in Los Angeles County, California, for example, function as pure provision units—through the so-called Lakewood Plan—although they have sufficient size to capture significant economies of scale from in-house production.[21]

Clearly, it is incorrect to assume that local governments that produce no services are inactive. On the provision side, these units may be very active indeed. Their activities include raising revenue, holding elections, deliberating on the needs of the community, choosing desired goods and services, determining levels of supply, shopping for service vendors of choice, negotiating contracts, and monitoring service flows. In very small units ordinary citizens do much of this work. Professional services, perhaps those of a planner or an engineer, a lawyer or an accountant, can also be employed as needed. *Lack of production does not indicate lack of performance.*

An additional question is whether "pure provision" has advantages on the provision side as well as on the production side. Most discussions of contracting focus on production-side advantages—the ability to produce services at lower cost; however, there may be important provision-side advantages as well. Anthony Downs has laid out such an argument in an essay titled "Separating the Planning and Procurement of Public Goods from Their Production and Delivery."[22] Planning and procurement are pro-vision-side activities. Downs argues that organizing production mainly in-house biases provision-side decisions in favor of producers. The interests of producers are commingled with those of consumers, resulting in provi-sion-side decisions that fail to represent consumer interests fully. The interests of producers and consumers are no more the same in the public sector as in the private sector. If those who are elected to represent citizens instead acquire a production-side perspective, production criteria come to dominate the decisions of provision units.

Downs does not apply this argument specifically to local government contracting. Clearly, however, a mayor or city manager in a pure provision unit serves a much different role than the same officer in a provision unit that organizes most service production in-house. In a pure provision unit, a chief administrative officer (CAO) performs a procurement function, rep-resenting the interests of consumers to producers. If, on the other hand, production is organized in-house, the CAO must fill two roles—represent-ing consumers and organizing production. An incentive to represent consumers may be weakened by the CAO's direct ties to production. Accountability would, in this case, be more easily obtained when provision units are free to represent the provision side exclusively.

It follows that contracting not only offers potential economies on the production side but also may enable provision units to perform provision functions more effectively. This argument can be contrasted to the more common argument made by critics of contracting—that one of the disad-vantages of contracting is a loss of direct control over production by public managers. If public managers are simply assumed to represent a public interest, then loss of direct control can be seen as disadvantageous. But to the extent that public managers reflect producer interests, loss of direct managerial control over production may actually enhance the representa-tion of citizen interests.

More research needs to be done to determine which view has greater accuracy. Public managers do not uniformly adopt a producer's perspective. A distinction needs to be made, for example, between department heads and central management. The characteristics of provision units, including size, heterogeneity, and form of government, may also have effects upon the perspective of a CAO. Is it possible for a public manager to decide even-handedly between in-house production and contracting, while maintaining both options? Neither should the possibility that contracting also offers provision-side advantages be dismissed. Pure provision units may have distinctive properties that deserve to be emulated rather than eliminated.

CONCLUSION

A considerable body of research suggests that separating provision and production potentially offers production-side advantages—obtaining greater efficiency from economies of scale for small provision units, helping to simplify public management in large provision units, and offering limited gains from producer competition. At the same time, there is also evidence to suggest that contracting-out works better in some circumstances than in others. Some services are more easily contracted-out due to the ease of measuring and monitoring performance. Gains from producer competition vary with the extent of the market, as well as the structure of the provision side; small metro areas, and to a greater degree rural areas, are less likely to realize gains from competition, although other advantages of contracting may be sufficient in the particular case. Moreover, contracting-out is no panacea: its utility depends greatly on provision-side performance, which depends, in turn, on how the provision side is organized.

In-house production continues to be prevalent, especially so among midsize municipalities.[23] What this means is not entirely clear. Although in St. Louis County pure provision units are limited to those so small that they would be unable to capture sufficient economies of scale to produce services in-house, in Los Angeles County they include midsize municipalities, fully capable of producing many services in-house. Public managers seem to face mixed incentives. The incentive of managers to shift the production of some services to outside vendors may be strongest when the efficiency gains from contracting can be captured for increased service production in-house. This suggests a producer bias on the part of public managers. "Pure provision" units, on the other hand, are relatively free of a producer bias.[24] Such units may afford the least distorted expression of consumer preferences possible in the public sector.

To *distinguish* provision and production conceptually is not necessarily to *separate* production from provision in practice. The major issue is whether contracting is a viable option, one not inherently inferior to in-house production. As long as production and delivery can be effectively monitored *and* as long as alternative producers are available (even if only the alternative of in-house production), both theory and research suggest that contracting is *at least equal* to in-house production as an option for linking provision to production. When providers are able to monitor production carefully, especially production outcomes for citizens, and when alternative producers are available, they gain leverage in their relationship with an existing producer, whether in-house or external. Theoretically, contracting offers the additional potential for reducing a producer bias among provision-side managers, thereby enhancing the representation of citizen-consumer interests. In sum, contracting-out appears to be neither an inherently superior alternative—one to be maximized—nor an inherently inferior alternative—one to be minimized. It is, rather, a viable option, whose net advantage or disadvantage depends on circumstances of time and place.

The viability of separating provision and production has important implications for the organization of local public economies, implications that extend well beyond contracting. If contracting is viable, provision-side organization need not be driven by production-related criteria. Rather, provision can be independently organized in ways best calculated to represent the interests of citizens, leaving the choice of production arrangement to case-by-case determination. Local public economies can therefore be expected to organize the provision side and the production side in substantially different ways. *Variety, not uniformity, should be the norm.* Even the decision to contract-out can be better understood in the full context of the variable provision and production arrangements available in a particular local public economy.

3

ORGANIZING
THE PROVISION SIDE

INTRODUCTION

DIFFERENT COMMUNITIES ORGANIZE PROVISION in different ways. To the extent that state and local rules allow, the provision side of a local public economy tends to be organized by a variety of provision units, small and large, overlapping in various ways. Some provision units are "nested" inside others, like municipalities within a county or villages within a township. Others have boundaries that cut across others in ways that invite comparison to a "crazy quilt." Such diversity contradicts the recommendations of orthodox reformers, who seek a more uniform set of provision units much fewer in number. To a considerable extent, the metropolitan-government movement has been driven by production concerns, an attempt to reduce waste and inefficiency in the delivery of services. If production can be separated from provision, however, production criteria need not drive the choice of provision units.

Provision-based criteria, such as the territorial distribution of preferences among citizens, can be major factors in determining the size and number of provision units, while production-based criteria, such as economies of scale, are satisfied on the production side. This can work because, as discussed in chapter 4, small provision units are able to draw on the capabilities of large production units, just as large provision units can do business with small production units. Examples of both abound.

Local public economies vary substantially in the extent of differentiation that exists among provision units. The types, size, and number of provision units all vary from one metro-area to another, especially among different states. The extent of differentiation is limited by two main factors:

(1) the rules that govern the formation of provision units and (2) the expected costs of organizing and operating an additional provision unit as compared to the expected benefits, benefits that derive mainly from the ability to tailor provision more precisely to the variety of local preferences. As discussed in chapter 1, these limits mean that provision units usually do not simply proliferate without reason.

This chapter examines various ways of organizing the provision side— assuming a capacity to organize the production side according to separate criteria. Provision-side organization makes use of multiple types of provision units—counties, townships, various types of municipalities, and a great variety of special districts. These units can be configured in many different ways. Although studies of governmental fragmentation in metropolitan areas usually lump together quite different configurations, provision-side inquiries should be concerned with studying the effects of different configurations on performance. Only in this way can the process of organizing provision be informed by relevant research.

TYPES OF PROVISION UNITS

The variety of potentially useful provision units is quite large and, very likely, not yet fully developed in practice. Traditional methods of classification, such as general-purpose versus special-purpose local governments, are inadequate for understanding the full range of possibilities. Provision units vary along a number of dimensions:

- Method of formation—whether public or private, with or without local discretion in adding a new unit
- Size of jurisdiction—measured by population
- Homogeneity of jurisdiction—one neighborhood, many neighborhoods, or areawide
- Scope of provision authority—the range of services a unit is authorized to provide
- Scope of provision—the range of services actually provided
- Coercive powers—taxing, zoning, other police powers, eminent domain
- Preemptive powers with respect to any provision units nested within it

It is important to describe provision units in terms of these multiple attributes rather than simply by their formal or legal name. Sometimes the legal name—city or village—is apt and descriptive, but often is not. Analyzing local governments on the basis of the *names of units* rather than their functional attributes—what they actually do—can lead to quite erroneous conclusions, especially concerning the oft-cited malady called "duplication of effort."

Default Units

It is useful first to distinguish between "default" units of local government and "optional" units created usually to supplement—occasionally to displace—the default unit.[1] The term "default" is used here as in a computer program: it denotes the primary unit of local government for any given community in the absence of action to create a different unit. As the term implies, no community is completely without local government. The typical default units in the U.S. are *counties* and *townships* (sometimes called towns). Both are usually supplied directly by state law (or constitution) and ordinarily are subdivisions of the state and therefore—at least originally— blanket its entire territory. The typical nondefault units are various sorts of *municipalities* and still more diverse *special-purpose districts*. Both are optional units, created by or for specific communities, seldom covering an entire state. Municipalities are considered "general-purpose" governments, though "multipurpose" is usually more descriptive (except perhaps those municipalities that organize the nation's largest cities). Both municipalities and special districts are ordinarily created to increase or augment the provisioning capabilities available through a default unit.

In many areas of the country townships have gradually lost their importance, superseded on the one hand by counties and on the other hand by optional municipalities, although the New England states are a major exception. In New England, the original default unit was the state (or colony), and townships were created only as communities were settled. West of the Appalachians, beginning in the Northwest Territory, townships were organized on a grid pattern, six miles square, without regard to patterns of settlement. In the South, townships were never organized, and counties served as the local default unit. Today, outside of New England, townships remain as important units of local government only in Pennsylvania, New Jersey, New York, and Wisconsin.[2]

Default units were organized to make provision for some minimal level of local services—a level likely to be demanded by any community. They therefore provide an institutional base on which other units are subsequently organized as needed. Counties were also organized to provide uniform statewide services on a decentralized basis, a function that they continue to perform even as their local-provision activities increase. Included among the typical responsibilities of counties are services such as public record-keeping, elections administration, and judicial administration including court and prosecutor (a function so fundamental, by the way, that the county seat of government is traditionally called the courthouse). Prior to the introduction of state police, county sheriffs, as officers of the court, were the principal agents of law enforcement throughout the state. The organization of counties is somewhat anomalous, inasmuch as most of the county officers responsible for producing and delivering state services (such as the sheriff) are locally elected. A unit of local government, accountable to local constituents, therefore substitutes for state bureaucracy. Townships have always been more locally oriented, in function as well as organization. However, township systems in which the township is not closely matched to a local settlement have gradually been eliminated or overshadowed by other units.

Optional Units

Municipalities are usually created as a supplement to (or in some cases a replacement of) default units. Included are units called cities, villages, and boroughs. Municipalities are created to provide additional increments or new types of services in those areas where local demand is greater (or in a few cases lesser).[3] Whether or not the default unit continues to exist, a municipality becomes the primary unit of local government in a community. There are numerous variations on the municipal theme. In New York State, for example, villages are nested inside townships, while cities replace township government but are nested inside counties. In Pennsylvania, both boroughs and cities, when organized, replace township government while remaining nested in counties, although townships have full municipal powers. In St. Louis County, Missouri, the "pure provision units" discussed in chapter 2 are mostly villages. Cities are normally divided into population classes for purpose of state legislation. Across the U.S. the size variation is enormous—from "cities" no bigger than villages to New York City, the nation's largest municipality covering five former counties now organized as subunits called boroughs.

The other major optional unit—special-purpose districts—are usually organized for one or two specific purposes, unlike both municipalities and the default units. Their diversity is even greater, considering that there is a type of special district for nearly any type of service provided by local government. School districts are the most numerous. It is useful to distinguish independent and dependent districts—the former must have their own taxing powers, while the latter are not counted in the Census of Governments. Districts, both independent and dependent, can be created either by local citizens, by some combination of petition and referendum, or by a parent government—county, township, or municipality. Independent district officials are often elected, but may be appointed by an overlying governmental unit. Dependent districts, formally at least, are little more than special taxing areas, but, informally, there may be substantial community-level participation in district decisions.

Counties, townships, municipalities, and special-purpose districts complement each other in important respects. A limiting factor in most municipal organization is that one municipality cannot overlap another—certainly not one municipality of the same type as the other. Cities are not nested inside cities; neither are villages nested inside villages. Counties and townships generally have the advantage of being able to *overlap* other types of units.[4] Thus cities and villages, as well as townships, are usually nested inside counties. A limiting factor in county and (outside New England) township organization is their typically inflexible and arbitrary boundaries, determined on a statewide basis rather than by local residents. Special districts have the twin virtues of being able to overlap other units, including other special districts, and of having flexible boundaries, often determined by local communities. Independent special districts can be used to differentiate provision in two ways: (1) varying the boundaries from those of a municipality, township, or county to accommodate a particular community of interest or (2) creating a redundant decision structure (such as a board of education) with boundaries coterminous with a general-purpose unit in order to make separate provision for a specific set of services.

The Special Case of Special Districts

The ACIR historically recommended limiting the use of special-purpose districts. In a 1964 report, *The Problem of Special Districts in American Government*, the Commission concluded that, in spite of their utility in filling institutional gaps among general-purpose governments in a locality, too many special districts had been created or allowed to continue when no longer needed. Since then, the number of special districts has increased by more than 60 percent, from 18,323 in 1962 to more than 30,000 at present (not including school districts). Although districts are used to provide virtually every conceivable local public service, they are more often associated with capital-intensive than labor-intensive services. The perceived disadvantages of special district governments included fiscal fragmentation, lack of accountability, and inefficient performance of services as compared to general-purpose governments.[5] In 1987, however, the ACIR altered its position. Recognizing that the *option* of special-purpose organization complements general-purpose units, and that the utility of the option is best judged on a case-by-case basis, the Commission recommended to the states that "no extraordinary limits and procedural burdens" be placed on the formation of special-purpose districts.[6]

If special districts are as defective as critics allege, the question is why citizens and their representatives choose to create and maintain them in such great numbers. Illinois and California have long led the nation in numbers of special districts, and studies conducted in both states have found positive results. In Illinois, a comprehensive study of special districts in Cook County, where the 196 districts included ninety-three organized to provide park services and forty-five to provide fire protection, concluded that their advantages outweigh their disadvantages to citizens.[7] In California, Robert B. Hawkins, Jr. found ample evidence that district governments fulfill a great variety of legitimate citizen demands that cannot be met satisfactorily through general-purpose governments.[8] Of course, the large and growing number of special districts adds substantially to governmental fragmentation thought to detract from metropolitan integration.

The creation of a district can sometimes be viewed as an effort to economize on the costs of operating additional provision units. Citizens may sometimes choose to create a special district within the boundaries of a default unit instead of organizing a municipality. If the citizen demand for services that justifies the organization of a new unit is limited in scope to one or two service areas—perhaps fire protection or sewers—then organizing a municipality would unnecessarily add to the cost of operating the new unit. Limiting the scope of action that may be taken can reduce the transaction costs of operating a provision unit. This is exactly what special district organization does—it limits, by statute, the scope of action that officials are authorized to undertake. The costs of both official decision making and citizen participation are then limited by law. The availability of the special-district option therefore enables citizens to obtain a more optimal set of provision units than if were they limited to general-purpose governments. States that severely constrain the creation of special districts limit citizens to less optimal forms of organization. Forcing local citizens to choose between no additional provision unit beyond the default unit and creating a new general-purpose government cannot increase efficiency on the provision side.

Municipalities also create special districts to provide services on a consolidated basis. Several municipalities may join, for example, to operate a wastewater treatment plant. Often, such districts are more nearly joint production units than provision units except that they may be self-financing through user fees.[9] Special districts thus offer an attractive alternative to the consolidation of general-purpose governments. If two adjacent municipalities are unable separately to provide for a single service that affects both, perhaps public transportation, requiring both municipalities to merge in order to provide a single service may distort the expression of citizen preferences for other services. Without the option of creating a special district, citizens are left with two decidedly suboptimal alternatives. Similarly, a special district can substitute for annexation by allowing a municipality, in effect, to extend its boundaries for provision of a single service. Again, eliminating the special-district option can only reduce provision-side efficiency, leading to a suboptimal result.

Districts are often useful in accommodating the actual shape of a public problem, matching the boundaries of the district to the boundaries of the problem. For example, numerous districts have been created to manage water resources—ground-water basins, surface watersheds, irrigation, and drainage.[10] The flexibility of district boundaries allows them to cross the boundaries of other governmental units, following instead the natural boundaries of the relevant resource system. In the absence of special-district government such problems are apt to be addressed by state or county bureaucracies, most likely in ways less sensitive to local variations. Special districts in these cases facilitate local problem solving, allowing a community of ground-water users or lakeside dwellers to act collectively to address a common problem.[11] The failure to facilitate local problem solving simply adds to the overcrowded agendas of state and federal governments and encourages less well-tailored solutions.

To some extent, districts have been used to circumvent onerous state restrictions on local government authority, especially debt restrictions. David L. Chicoine and Norman Walzer argue that this may have been the case in Illinois. They cite, in support of the proposition, a finding that counties in which a larger percentage of the population lives in home-rule municipalities (with no tax and debt limits imposed by state statute) tend to have fewer taxing units per 10,000 residents.[12] Statutory tax and debt limits that do not allow local citizens to approve increases beyond those limits can distort the provision of local public goods. If special districts offer local communities a route of escape, the limits also distort the structure of the local public economy. Special districts created to avoid such restrictions do not necessarily have other advantages that would lead to their creation, and local citizens are being forced to suboptimize. The remedy for this situation, however, is not to limit the formation of special districts, but to remove overly restrictive limitations on local government authority.[13]

Special districts vary in their relationships to other units of government. The principal reference in this section has been to "independent" districts, which have substantial autonomy guaranteed by their power to tax. "Dependent" districts, those without the power to tax and therefore not counted as governments, are often created by the action of other units rather than directly by citizens, and in some cases they are managed by those other units, though not always. Although most school districts are independent, even dependent school districts possess considerable autonomy, often lacking only final approval of a budget and a separate tax levy. The most limited type of dependent district is formally no more than a separate taxing area. The district allows a separate tax rate to be levied for taxpayers within its boundaries, with the revenues earmarked for provision of a specific service supplied only within the district. Although they lack autonomous decision making, and district authority is vested in the parent governmental body, tax districts can effectively be used to attain better fiscal equivalence, one of the key ingredients of provision-side efficiency. Some default units, in contrast to municipalities, are inclined to create special tax districts in large numbers. For example, by 1985, New York State's 932 townships (called "towns") had created a total of 6,859 districts,[14] located mostly in metropolitan areas. Such a large number of tax districts indicate an extraordinary commitment in town government to fiscal equivalence. As long as citizens find them responsive to their local interests, tax districts are the most economical provision unit—in terms of transaction costs—that can be created.[15]

Kathryn A. Foster recently published a useful study of special districts in metropolitan areas based on census data.[16] One of her principal conclusions is that special districts tend to spend more money per capita than general-purpose governments. A closer look at her findings, however, reveals a mixed picture. Four types of districts—airport, transit, water, and fire protection districts—spend no more than general-purpose governments on their respective functions after controlling for per capita income and population size at the metropolitan level. Other types of districts do tend to spend more, including districts related to ports, utilities, sewers, natural resources, libraries, parks and recreation, and housing and community development. Unmeasured demand-side variables may nevertheless still account for many of these findings. The economic demand for housing and community development, for example, often originates from outside a metropolitan area, supported by intergovernmental grants; per capita income in the Metropolitan Statistical Area (MSA) would not pick that up. In some cases, special districts may be more entrepreneurial and responsive to consumer demand and thus spend more: this is particularly true, for example, of parks and recreation districts, many of whose programs are funded from user fees. Districts formed to manage natural resources respond not to income effects but to resource-management problems, such as the depletion of groundwater or the management of a forest or lake.

Foster also reports that districts tend to make larger capital investments in similar functions than do general-purpose governments, in addition to spending more on operations and maintenance. One interpretation of this finding is that district decision making exhibits a bias toward capital projects, thus increasing total spending. An alternative interpretation is that local officials contemplating large capital investments tend to form special districts to manage those investments. Why? In order to protect the long-term value of the investment from short-term political incentives to shirk on maintenance.[17] Orthodox public administration literature has historically portrayed special-purpose governments as an alternative inherently inferior to general-purpose governments. Sometimes, though rarely, the more zealous advocates of special districts have perhaps argued for their inherent superiority. Foster's findings rather clearly point away from both extremes. Special-purpose districts, like contracting and other less orthodox instruments of local government, are neither inherently inferior or superior, but are potentially useful provision arrangements that may also, on occasion, be subject to abuse.

The number of special districts, or their rate of growth, affords no evidence of poor performance. In fact, the opposite may be true. Citizens often create special districts by means of local referenda as provided by state enabling legislation. Presumably they would not do so unless they expect the new unit to perform better than existing units for the specific purpose at hand. To be sure, all special districts are not equally worthwhile, and the citizens and officials who create such districts can and do make mistakes. Yet each district should be evaluated on the basis of its performance as a provision unit within a local public economy, focusing especially on its contribution to the representation of citizen interests as consumers of public goods and services. A general bias against special districts is hardly warranted given the numerous ways in which districts can complement general-purpose governments. The rapid growth in the number of special districts very likely reflects this complementarity.

At the same time, there is reason for caution in the study and assessment of districts. Special districts include a wide variety in size, function, and means of governance. While they are not inherently inferior to general-purpose governments, neither should they be viewed as inherently superior. In some cases, large countywide or metro-wide districts have been created to preempt more localized provision of services such as water and sewer, creating a single monopoly provider responsible for a very diverse set of local conditions and circumstances. In other cases, citizens use special districts to resist the imposition of monopoly providers. When a category is a diverse as special-purpose government—ranging from the Port Authority of New York to the local cemetery district—it is extraordinarily difficult to investigate "the effects" of special districts. The answer is often "it depends," for the effects of districts will vary with context—the surrounding local public economy and the rules by which it is organized.

Neighborhood Units: "Lilliputs," RCAs, and BIDs

Critics frequently denigrate small units of local government—especially those under 1,000 population—as "toy governments," "postage stamp governments," "peanut governments," or "lilliputs," as if the term "government" should be identified with grander concerns than maintaining the livability of a neighborhood that contains several hundred households. The legal nomenclature is often no help. Fourth-class "cities" in Missouri, for example, have a maximum size of 3,000 people. Sometimes the legal nomenclature does help, distinguishing "villages" from cities, for example, but often analysts ignore such distinctions. If the government of a "city" of 1,000 residents attempted to function as a city of 100,000, such a city would not be economically viable. A residential community of 1,000 people located in a metropolitan area is not a city, however; it more closely approximates a neighborhood.

A disparity between name and function does not make small municipalities insignificant. Once the legal nomenclature is set aside, neighborhood governments can be recognized in large numbers outside central cities, although the total population of such units is often not sufficient to include a large percentage of the metropolitan area. The villages and tiny "cities" of metropolitan America are neighborhoods with their own neighborhood governments. Nested within metropolitan counties, most can operate effectively (as discussed in chapter 2) as pure provision units.

Neighborhood governments have a private analog in the organization of residential community associations (RCAs),[18] the most rapidly growing type of local provision unit in the country.[19] Residential subdivisions, when collectively organized by homeowners associations, are able to function as collective provision units. Homeowners associations are privately organized, initially by developers, who create the association by attaching membership and fee requirements as deed covenants when each separate parcel is sold. Thus, the association exists and operates as a matter of private rather than public law. Residents become members of the association upon acquiring title to property just as they become citizens of a municipality upon taking up residence within its boundaries. Although legally private, an organized subdivision is functionally equivalent to a municipality—at least with respect to homeowners. RCAs are able to make collective provision for local public goods and services through mandatory assessments on homeowners, not unlike property taxes. The principal institutional difference between an RCA and a local government is the difference between property ownership as a criterion of membership and residence as a criterion of municipal citizenship. With membership in an RCA comes a legal obligation to pay association dues, as well as rights to participate in decisions, either directly or through an elected board. Unlike many local governments, of course, nearly all RCAs are neighborhood units.

Sometimes characterized as "private governments," RCAs are perhaps better understood as "common property" institutions.[20] Common property is private property held in common. It has similarities to public property, except that ownership is vested in a group of private individuals, not in a governmental unit. Common property associations face a set of characteristic problems related to the management of their common interests. These include exclusion of nonmembers, regulation of joint use, and the ability to make and enforce collective decisions. RCAs have developed various ways of addressing each of these problems. In St. Louis County, Missouri, for example, more than 400 "private-street associations"[21] have been formed by means of trust-indentures, which mandate the creation of a board of trustees to be elected by homeowners, and the payment of subdivision fees by homeowners, usually assessed on a flat rate or frontage basis. Nonpayment becomes a lien on the property, providing an enforcement mechanism. Private street associations can and do limit street access, closing and barricading streets that would open their residential communities to arterial traffic, while providing a full range of residential street services as determined by residents, including street and sidewalk repair, cleaning, snow removal, lighting, mowing, and trimming.[22] More generally, RCAs are able to enforce deed covenants that restrict property use within the community, using powers somewhat analogous to municipal zoning but employed at neighborhood discretion.[23]

Private St. Louis street associations successfully use a common property arrangement to provide local streets and related services and at the same time protect their communities from the ill effects of high traffic volume— eroding the quality of life in residential settings. This particular organization of a neighborhood commons suggests that common property may have a broader contribution to make to urban organization. Much of the dynamic of urban decline at the street level resembles the well-known "tragedy of the commons," a model ordinarily used to explain the deterioration of natural resources. The tragedy occurs when the individual users of a shared resource or facility (such as a common pasture in the classic illustration), acting separately for their individual benefit, bring ruin to all by destroying the resource on which all depend. As Jane Jacobs recognized in her classic study, *The Death and Life of Great American Cities*,[24] streets define complex open spaces—an urban commons—subject to joint use by diverse users within limits or tolerances. When the limits are exceeded, some residents are unable to cope, and a dynamic of neighborhood decline sets in.

It is now well established that when resource users own a resource in common and are able to act collectively, the tragedy of the commons can be avoided.[25] Public ownership of resources, by contrast, has often led to a perpetual "open season" on their use and abuse, due to inappropriate regulations or inadequate enforcement. Similarly, large municipal governments sometimes virtually abandon street neighborhoods that become too difficult to control. Conventional urban organization is predicated on a public-private dichotomy: private property owners tend to separable interests, while the common interests they share are the responsibility of local governments. RCAs do not fit the public-private dichotomy. As common-property institutions, private in some ways, public in others, they offer capabilities that may be useful in stemming urban decline.

Theoretically, the principal advantage offered by RCAs is based on incentives. Large-scale municipalities rely on the incentives of government officials to protect a great variety of street-neighborhoods, while RCAs rely on the incentives of property owners to protect their particular street-neighborhoods. Common property brings private incentives to bear on common interests. Paul Peterson, among others, has argued persuasively that the protection of property values is at the root of local government behavior.[26] Yet local government institutions may differ markedly in their ability to translate such incentives into collective action. Local property owners do have substantial incentives to protect their property values. Compared to city hall, street-level common property institutions can more directly translate private incentives into collective action. If the definition of a property "owner" is expanded to include licensed street vendors and apartment lessors, both of whom can be understood as owning an interest in the street, then the capacity to protect street-level interests can be strengthened still further.

Many, perhaps most, urban streets are unlikely candidates for common property organization—owned by adjacent property owners—due to arterial use and the need to be responsive to interests outside the immediate neighborhood. Sidewalks are, however, another matter, as are alleys and neighborhood parks. In terms of the public-private dichotomy, the transfer of these facilities to local property owners would amount to the privatization of urban space. Common property, however, is not fully "private" in all that the term connotes. Common property is used to organize the joint use of common facilities, not the individual use of separate facilities. It is protective of common, not purely individualistic, interests. Although sure to be considered a radical idea by many, this step can be viewed as a natural extension of the now-familiar concept of a condominium into the wider organization of an urban neighborhood, already well developed among apartment communities in Seoul, Korea.[27]

Action by the owners of common property occurs on the *provision side* of a local public economy. Homeowners or property-owners associations need not *produce* services. In fact, municipal governments are frequently among the producers of services supplied to RCAs. The basic problem of urban organization, however, is on the provision-side. This is where RCAs can be expected primarily to operate—in many if not most cases as pure provision units.

Recent trends indicate significant movement in the direction of RCA/common-property organization within large American cities. One of the most promising developments is the creation of Business Improvement Districts (BIDs) to provide auxiliary public services in commercial neighborhoods.[28] For example, fifty-three BIDs now operate in New York State, thirty-three of them in New York City with several more proposed.[29] Similar to special-purpose districts, BIDs are authorized by state enabling legislation as a supplementary unit, but are closely tied, like RCAs, to property owners within the district. The result is a mandatory association of property owners, created by the city at neighborhood initiative, governed by its members, and financed through a special property-tax levy. Unlike most special-purpose districts, however, BIDs usually provide a variety of services, such as street and sidewalk cleaning and repair, auxiliary police, parking facilities, beautification, and street lighting, as well as development projects. Like other optional (nondefault) units, BIDs supplement the capabilities supplied by the base unit, in this case usually a municipality. Concerned about urban deterioration in commercial areas, state legislatures are turning to those with the greatest incentive to reverse the trend—the owners of commercial property.[30]

RCAs can usually be created only at the point of initial housing development. Individual homeowners then agree to membership in the association when they buy property in the subdivision. In an already established neighborhood the formation of a private, voluntary association would require unanimous consent among the homeowners. Unanimity rules create incentives for some individuals to act as holdouts,[31] precluding RCA formation. To create an RCA in an established neighborhood would probably require a formation rule less inclusive than unanimity. This can only be supplied by state law. In form, it would become a neighborhood government, limited in its scope of authority to those activities deemed appropriate for neighborhood provision. BIDs provide an important model for creating self-governing districts in residential neighborhoods as well. Numerous neighborhood government proposals have envisioned the creation of neighborhood subunits on a boilerplate" basis throughout a city—not unlike the creation of townships in the Old Northwest Territory. Such an approach would give every "neighborhood" a neighborhood government, whether or not it wanted one. The BID model views neighborhood government as an optional—nondefault—unit. Neighborhood units would then be formed only where citizens have judged that the benefits outweigh the costs.

One difficulty with the BID model, at least as designed in New York State, is the requirement of *municipal action* to create the BID. Municipalities—referring to nondefault units such as cities and villages—historically have tended to preempt the organization of supplementary provision units within municipal boundaries, creating a monopoly in provision. Large cities that preempt the organization of supplementary units may have difficulty responding to the diverse interests of neighborhoods. This may help to explain both the high costs and poor service quality frequently observed in central cities. Longstanding proposals to allow the formation of neighborhood governments would increase the potential variety of provision units with central cities,[32] but neighborhood governments have been notoriously difficult to create *within* large incorporated municipalities. The difficulty derives from the "rules of the game," insofar as municipal incorporation generally preempts any further public incorporation without the consent of the municipality. Neighborhoods are not permitted to incorporate as "villages" within an already incorporated "city." The rule derives from a view of municipal government that sees a municipality as *properly* a monopolist within its sphere, an idea that has long inhibited the development of a more differentiated local public economy within large central cities. In the suburbs, a highly differentiated local public economy is able to develop because county government, as a default unit, does not generally preempt municipal incorporation.

BIDs represent an important step toward the development of a more highly differentiated public economy within central cities. The next step needed is to extend BID-type arrangements to residential communities. The full development of neighborhood districts may depend, however, on autonomous neighborhood incorporation powers, directly analogous to municipal incorporation, that do not require the consent of the overlying municipal jurisdiction to incorporate. Incorporated neighborhoods would then be authorized by state law to raise revenue and take other actions appropriate to their functions, just like other units of local government.

In 1967 the ACIR recommended that states authorize large cities and county governments in metropolitan areas to establish "neighborhood subunits" with limited functional and taxing powers.[33] The term "subunit" was carefully chosen. Cities and counties would be authorized, not required, to create these entities, and could dissolve them at will. Subunits of existing local governments were distinguished from new local units that would exacerbate perceived problems of urban "fragmentation." BIDs tend to be subunits in this sense, but they are subunits with a lot of autonomy. In 1985 the Commission renewed its recommendation, urging the use of neighborhood subunits in distressed communities, but omitting reference to dissolution and adding the possibility of creation through initiative and referendum procedures.[34] The latter would allow for direct creation by citizens, much like municipal incorporation. The key is a state statute (or in some few cases, perhaps, a municipal charter provision) that specifies (1) a procedure by which *citizens* can act to create a neighborhood unit on their own motion and (2) the substantive powers and duties of such a unit once created. The latter should include, at a minimum, power to raise revenue, receive revenue by transfer, perform services under contract, and accept functional responsibility by transfer from an overlying jurisdiction.[35]

SIZE AND PERFORMANCE

One dimension on which provision units vary widely is size, measured by population. The public problems to which service provision responds also appear in a variety of sizes and shapes, embracing discrete populations of various sizes. A well-structured local public economy is one that matches the size of provision units to the size of the problems being addressed. Problems best addressed on a small scale are assigned to relatively small provision units, while problems best addressed on a larger scale go to larger units. Evidence of such matching can be found in the more highly differentiated local public economies.

In St. Louis County, for example, street service provision tends to be divided among three types of units: (1) small municipalities and private subdivisions, (2) larger municipalities, and (3) county government.[36] The first group provides for residential streets with priority attention to the control of traffic flow. The second group is more heterogeneous in its scope of provision, but often leaves residential streets to subdivisions, concentrating on streets with higher traffic volume. The third unit, county government, provides for a countywide arterial street system. Small units provide for small-scale interests, while large units provide for large-scale interests that lie beyond the scope of neighborhood-level organizations. The result is a set of nested provision units that simultaneously give attention to a mixed set of priorities. Only the unincorporated portion of the county departs substantially from the threefold division of responsibility, county government providing for most street services (except state highways). However, increased demand for municipal incorporation in this area has been fueled in part by street-service concerns—traffic congestion and control.

In the field of public education, regular elementary and secondary schools are maintained in St. Louis County by twenty-three separate school districts, while special education is provided through a countywide special district. The logic of countywide provision is based on the nature of the specific service being provided. Given the higher cost of special education, a local school district that attempts to provide high-quality service would attract residents in need of those services. This would drive up the tax-price of public education in such a district compared to others. The ability of residents to relocate among districts could lead to a dynamic that would depress the quality of special education throughout the area. The nature of the service makes it difficult to make separate local provision for special education within a metropolitan housing market. A countywide district is better to aggregate the demand for special education and foster an appropriate level of provision. Yet the same considerations do not apply to regular instruction, nor do they apply to the "production" of special education, which tends to be a joint undertaking between the special district and regular districts (see chapter 4).

Wide variation also exists in the size of provision units used to provide the same services. Some local public economies exhibit much less differentiation than others, or have developed unevenly. This raises the possibility that some provision responsibilities may not be well matched to existing provision units. One service area that has been carefully studied in this regard is police protection. Elinor Ostrom and colleagues at the Workshop in Political Theory and Policy Analysis, Indiana University, have conducted extensive studies to determine the effect of jurisdictional size on citizen evaluations of police, among other measures of police performance. The Workshop studies consistently demonstrate that *smaller* units tend to be *more responsive* providers of police patrol services. The research program included the study of police services in a number of metropolitan areas, consistently focusing on the delivery of services in relatively similar neighborhoods by police departments of varying size, ranging from a few part-time officers to more than 2,000 officers. As performance measures, the studies used indicators such as victimization rates, whether citizens call police when victimized, speed of response when victimized, and general citizen evaluations of police. None of these studies found a large police department (over 350 officers) able to perform more effectively in delivering direct services to citizens in similar neighborhoods than smaller departments. Frequently, small departments deliver better service at lower cost.[37]

The Workshop studies could not sort out the effects of relatively small-scale provision from small-scale production, this because most small municipal police departments both provide and produce police patrol services (see chapter 4). However, the principal explanation offered for the findings—an explanation consistent with the data—can be viewed as a provision-side explanation, namely, that smaller departments place a greater percentage of sworn officers on the street than larger departments. In other words, smaller municipalities assign a *higher priority* to street patrol than do larger municipalities. The assignment of priorities among various services (or service components) is a *provision function*, one intended to reflect the preferences of citizens. Smaller police departments receive better evaluations from citizens for patrol service because the officials of small municipalities assign a higher priority to patrol. Police patrol, much like the care of residential streets noted above, is a small-scale problem, one best provided for by small-scale provision units. Theory and evidence coincide on this point.

Other scholars have studied the relationship between *school district* size and pupil performance. School *districts* are provision units, while schools are production units. Most school districts, except for the very smallest, organize and operate a number of schools. This was not always the case. The number of independent school districts has decreased from more than 128,000 in 1932 to less than 15,000 today. School-district consolidation is the only successful consolidation movement in the U.S., and consolidation efforts continue. The argument for consolidation has generally rested on suggested links between larger district size and various intervening variables, such as spending per pupil, larger facilities, and more extensive curricula, each connected to pupil performance. However, the consolidation argument can be reinterpreted in terms of the assignment of priorities among service components. Larger districts were *expected* to assign higher priority to physical facilities and curricular diversity. This in turn was *expected* to lead to higher pupil performance. Research suggests that the opposite may have happened.

A study of 97 school districts in New York State found that, controlling for expenditure levels and the family background of students, pupil performance on standardized tests declined as size of district increased.[38] Similarly, a California study found that school district size (beyond a minimum threshold) had a consistent negative effect on various measures of student achievement.[39] Using a sample of 144 unified school districts (those providing both elementary and secondary education) with student populations of 2,000 or more, researchers found that students in larger districts tended to have lower scores on standardized achievement tests. This research controlled for the effects of family poverty, minority background, and community wealth as measured by median student IQ scores and expenditures per student.[40] Although neither study suggests that district size is the major explanatory factor—this honor goes to student social background—the research does bring into question the premise of the consolidation movement.

The results of the school district studies have not yet been satisfactorily explained. One possibility, however, is that consolidationists were correct in their expectations with respect to altered priorities, but that these are the wrong priorities. Smaller school districts may place a higher priority on other aspects of the education service, such as school-to-parent relationships and teacher-pupil interactions. Educators increasingly view these more subtle and less easily measured dimensions of education as important. These dimensions may also be the among the highest priorities of parents and, thus, are better reflected in small, community-based school districts. This is at least a theoretical account congruent with the available research. Further research is needed to confirm this explanation or another.

Smaller is not always better. Sanitary wastewater services provide an example in which provision by a relatively small unit fails to assign the correct priority, leading to higher costs to users. A study in DuPage County, Illinois, a metropolitan county just west of Chicago's Cook County, compared *local provision of wastewater collection* with *regional provision of collection* in a context where treatment provision is regional.[41] "Collection" refers to the construction and maintenance of sewer lines that transport wastewater to treatment plants. In both cases, a regional provision unit (either a special district or the county government) is providing treatment. In one case collection is provided separately by each municipality nested within the boundaries of the regional agency; in the other case collection is provided by the same regional agency that provides treatment. In this context, regional agencies that provide treatment assign a higher priority to sewer line maintenance than do local municipalities. Why? Because the effects of poor maintenance are initially experienced at the treatment plant in higher costs of treatment. Badly maintained sewer lines permit water to flow through the lines, increasing the costs of treating the flow. The regional treatment provider passes these higher costs on to users, while the local municipality appears to operate at lower cost. The incentive to maintain sewer lines at an optimal level of performance lies with the treatment provider. Between these two arrangements, one that *differentiates* provision of treatment and collection and the other that *integrates* provision of treatment and collection, integrated provision by a regional unit was associated with lower total costs to users.[42]

Provision-functions with respect to the *same* service need not be vested in a single unit. Sometimes *co-provision* makes sense. The provision of public education, for example, is usually shared in the United States between each state and its local school districts. An economic rationale for this sort of arrangement is the existence of externalities or spillover effects. When a provision unit is organized to represent the interests of immediate beneficiaries—who directly receive services—the level of provision may affect others outside the basic provision unit. Grants-in-aid that transfer funds from more inclusive to less inclusive provision units give fiscal expression to the interests of others outside the basic provision unit. This allows larger, more inclusive communities to buy into and support provision by smaller, local communities. The local unit, such as a school district, however, must take responsibility of arranging for production and perhaps organizing its own production unit.

Other possibilities exist for dividing and sharing the distinct functions of provision. Municipalities (or other more inclusive units) sometimes contract with neighborhood units to deliver services within their own neighborhoods. This arrangement may increase the accountability of producers to the neighborhood, not because of municipal provision activity, but because the neighborhood organization is able to function, formally or informally, to represent the interests of neighborhood residents—a provision function. Such an arrangement makes economic sense when economies of scale in production are limited and when the larger unit is willing and better able to finance provision (e.g., social services).

HOW MUCH DIFFERENTIATION IS ENOUGH?

The amount of differentiation among provision units—the number and variety that can economically be created and operated—is limited, as discussed in chapter 1, by the costs of organizing and operating additional units. General-purpose units are sometimes preferred because they enable citizens to obtain a wide range of goods and services while economizing on the costs of organizing and operating provision units; yet special-purpose units can also be more economical when citizens want a more limited range of services. In general, greater differentiation can better accommodate diversity but only at the price of making a greater investment in public transactions. Citizens need multiple organizational options in order to create a local public economy that reflects appropriate trade-offs.

In more orthodox terms, differentiation is "fragmentation." An empirical literature focusing upon the fiscal effects of both "fragmentation" and overlapping jurisdictions has developed in recent decades, mostly among public finance economists. Generally, this line of research has found *lower* levels of local government expenditure to be associated with *higher* levels of fragmentation and overlap, even when controlling for the level of community demand for local public goods and services. Cross-sectional research by Richard E. Wagner and Warren E. Weber,[43] Thomas Dilorenzo,[44] and Mark Schneider[45] all point consistently in the same direction. Dilorenzo employed a measure of "concentration," the degree to which tax or expenditure efforts are concentrated in the four largest jurisdictions (of whatever type) in a county for specific services, and found that concentration is associated with higher expenditure levels for the county as a whole. Schneider looked at fragmentation as measured more traditionally—number of municipalities per 100,000 residents in an urban county—and explicitly controlled for the level of municipal demand for local public goods and services. The latter is important; if a variety of provision units are more demand-responsive, this can lead either to greater or lesser government expenditure. Using a demand-side model, Schneider observed a negative sign between fragmentation and growth in expenditures over a five-year period.[46]

With reference specifically to police services, Workshop studies[47] found that the number of police jurisdictions per 100,000 population is strongly and negatively related to per capita expenditures for police in a nationwide sample of metropolitan areas. The greater the number of jurisdictions in a metropolitan area, the less they tend to spend for policing in the aggregate. Controlling for the service quality ratings of suburban respondents (the great majority of jurisdictions being suburban) strengthens the negative relationship, indicating that the higher expenditures found in less fragmented areas do not reflect higher service quality, at least not in the minds of citizen-consumers.

A few studies have attempted to examine the relationship between fragmentation and overall citizen satisfaction with services or with local government generally. Overall citizen satisfaction is multidimensional; it can include satisfaction with this but dissatisfaction with that. The major difficulty with this line of work is a reliance on *summary indicators* of citizen satisfaction that cannot reflect its multidimensional character. A North Carolina study used statistical scaling techniques to collapse citizen evaluations of services into a single indicator.[48] Then, using counties as units of analysis, the study found that county fragmentation was negatively related to service quality. Use of the scaling technique, however, may eliminate important information from analysis, as may the aggregation of citizens by counties. An Illinois study used similar techniques to study counties (excluding Cook County) and found similar results using a single scale of service perception.[49] The researchers suggest that this result does not support the idea that smaller units of government are more responsive to citizen preferences. Aggregating citizen evaluations by county, however, does not permit a direct examination of this question. Even in counties with a very large number of provision units, it is often true that most citizens reside in jurisdictions that are relatively large. To date, the most ambitious effort to examine the relationship between fragmentation and satisfaction is the work of William Lyons, David Lowery, and Ruth Hoogland DeHoog in Kentucky.[50] Their studies compare five matched pairs of communities in and Lexington/Fayette County and Jefferson County outside Louisville. Lexington is a well-known city-county consolidation, while Jefferson County is a fragmented metropolitan county. Using a single, straightforward indicator of citizen satisfaction with their local government, they report no consistent difference between the two counties. Unfortunately, their work takes no account of service costs, except as an unmeasured dimension of satisfaction.

When analyzing discrete services, the Illinois study (cited above) found mixed results. Citizen perceptions of education and parks[51] were favorably affected by fragmentation, while highways and libraries were unfavorably affected. The research concludes that different patterns of organization may be appropriate for different types of services. This conclusion in general *supports* the idea of differentiating the provision of local goods and services. Summary indicators of citizen satisfaction, such as used in the comparative studies in North Carolina and Kentucky, fail to capture this important information.

The weight of evidence supports the proposition that, in general, differentiated provision (fragmentation) reduces local government costs. This does not imply, however, that any particular pattern of differentiation is well designed. In fact, equally fragmented metropolitan areas are often structured in very different ways,[52] limiting the validity of research that pits highly fragmented areas against consolidated areas. One important variable among fragmented areas is the presence and treatment of unincorporated territory. In Pennsylvania, for example, unincorporated territory is nonexistent. In many other states, metropolitan areas include unincorporated territory in which county government functions as the default unit. St. Louis County, even though it has some ninety municipalities, has a large unincorporated area. If unincorporated territory is organized with reference to special tax districts, fiscal equivalence can be maintained. If not, residents of incorporated areas may provide substantial subsidies to unincorporated residents. Likewise, consolidated metropolitan areas exhibit differences. UNIGOV in Indianapolis, Indiana, permits existing suburban municipalities to continue in existence, providing local services including police. Lexington/Fayette County, Kentucky, utilizes dependent tax districts to maintain fiscal equivalence.[53]

In addition to asking *how much* differentiation there is, we need to ask *what kind* there is. Alternative patterns of differentiation depend on the rules that govern the establishment and operation of provision units. Some patterns are surely more optimal than others. The theoretical prediction is that efficiency and satisfaction are associated with optimality, not a greater or lesser number of provision units. Future research needs to take account of the rules used to organize the provision side—the terms and conditions for creating provision units—as a way of explaining the varieties of fragmentation.[54] This topic is discussed further in chapter 5.

CONCLUSION

The various types and sizes of local governments in the United States are specialized to various dimensions of public service provision. One dimension is spatial, reflecting, on the one hand, the diversity of preference clusters among local residents and, on the other hand, the nature of the service—the field of effects associated with provision or nonprovision. Another dimension is functional, sorting out preferences with respect to one service from preferences for another service. In some cases citizens join only with their immediate neighbors to provide certain services, while in other cases citizens combine with others throughout a metropolitan area to make provision for their common interests. As local public economies develop, both the number and the variety of provision units grow. Relatively new neighborhood provision units, such as RCAs and BIDs, hold out considerable promise as viable means for accommodating small communities of interest often left unattended by much larger provision units, especially central cities. The result is greater differentiation on the provision side, entailing an increase in governmental fragmentation. It is unlikely that local and metropolitan problem solving will lead to a decrease in the number of local governments. As for size, both small and large units have an important place in provision-side organization.

Governmental fragmentation can neither be wholly condemned nor unconditionally welcomed in metropolitan America. Yet while more research remains to be done, the relative efficiency of maintaining a variety and multiplicity of provision units in a metropolitan area has been well established, taking account of both service costs and citizen satisfaction with discrete services. Although it would be incorrect—both theoretically and empirically—to claim that more differentiated provision is always better than less, what theory and research do show is that more differentiated provision *can be* and frequently *is* better than less. The use of differentiated provision units clearly serves important and legitimate purposes.

Perhaps the key issue in organizing the provision side is who gets to choose among alternative organizational arrangements. One approach is to give *citizens* a wide range of organizational options and let them choose, empowering citizens to combine in various ways to act collectively and make the relevant trade-offs. This idea is explored more fully in chapter 5, but first, chapter 4 takes up the problem of organizing the production side of a local public economy.

④

ORGANIZING
THE PRODUCTION SIDE

INTRODUCTION

EVERY PROVISION UNIT MUST decide how to arrange for production, and each one may do so somewhat differently. As provision units choose among alternative production arrangements, they generate the production side of the local public economy. The resulting organization of the production side is likely to involve many different production arrangements responsive to diverse criteria—specialization, economies (and diseconomies) of scale, and competition. It is impossible to know *a priori*—without specific time-and-place information—what set of arrangements will be more nearly optimal. In other words, there is no one right way to organize the production side in all times and places. As discussed in chapter 2, distinguishing provision and production does not necessarily imply the need to separate production from provision. Most provision units, except for small neighborhood units, choose to organize *some* aspect of production in-house. Yet rarely do provision units organize *all* aspects of production in-house, leading to complex production arrangements that include both large-scale and small-scale agencies, each specialized to different tasks.

The focus of this chapter is not upon the organization of production within production units but upon the distribution of production tasks among independent units within service sectors—focusing on police, fire, education, and street sectors. Each service consists of multiple "components," separate tasks that contribute to its delivery. *Service delivery* is analogous to *product assembly*—each depends on the production of separate components. In both cases, production tasks often vary sharply among different components. If one service component is labor intensive, while

59

another is capital intensive, economies of scale are likely to differ between the two. As in the case of product assembly, often it is more efficient to organize production by relying on independent units to produce different service components. This chapter examines four service sectors in two metro areas. It demonstrates that highly differentiated production arrangements that make good economic sense can and do emerge from the decisions of multiple provision units in a local public economy.

SERVICE SECTORS

The key to understanding the organization of service production in local public economies is the choice of units of analysis—the conceptual building blocks for understanding any system of organization. Conventionally, the basic unit of analysis in local public administration is a department or agency nested within a local government. In a study of police services, for example, municipal police departments become the basic unit of analysis. Production at the metropolitan level is measured by simply aggregating departmental data. The use of this unit of analysis presumes, however, that service production is mostly self-contained within departments. If it is not, the conclusions are erroneous and misleading. To understand service production at the metropolitan level it is necessary to focus on patterns of organization *among* departments and agencies. This requires a different unit of analysis: the *service sector*.

The production side of a local public economy is best understood as a collection of multiple service sectors. Each major service sector, be it police, fire protection, street services, solid waste, water and sewer, education, libraries, parks and recreation, transportation, or human services, tends to exhibit different patterns of organization. Departments or agencies fit inside sectors, and each one can only be understood in terms of its role in a sector. Each sector coordinates the production of several distinct but complementary *service-components*, different components presenting somewhat different production tasks. Typically, a service sector consists of several types of agencies, each one specialized in the production of a different service-component or closely related set of components. A police services sector, for example, is ordinarily composed of police departments, dispatch centers, forensic units, specialized detective squads, and a training academy. Sectors differ, however, in the degree to which the production of various tasks is distributed among a variety of agencies or concentrated in one or a few. Variation occurs both across service types and between regions.

The *structure of the sector* derives from the extent to which production is differentiated across service-components, measured by the number and size of producers for various service components. The principal cause of differentiation is variation in economies of scale. Some service-components benefit from larger scale production, while other components either do not so benefit or require a smaller scale of production. Production may be separated from provision for some service-components—as discussed in chapter 2—but not for others. In addition, some service-components may be produced by tens or hundreds of agencies while other components are produced by only one or two agencies—all within the same metropolitan service sector.

Production *efficiency*, in particular, is an attribute of service sectors, not simply of separate agencies, and it depends on the structure of the sector. The ability to produce services efficiently depends on organizing a sector that takes advantage of *diverse* economies of scale, scale considerations that vary across production components. For this reason, sectors may often concentrate some service-components in a small number of large-scale agencies while distributing other components among a large number of small-scale agencies. These are in fact the sectors that tend to achieve the highest levels of efficiency across different services.

Scale refers here to the population of the service area. Instead of counting the number of units of output produced, the scale of public service production is usually measured by the size of the population served. A large-scale agency in this context is one that serves a large population; it is not necessarily "large" measured by number of employees. Size in the latter sense, however, is also relevant to the efficiency of public service production.

The first step in analyzing a service sector is to identify the different service-components that are needed to produce a service. Each component is a necessary element in a coordinated system of production. For example, police services include patrolling, dispatching, investigating, and training as production components. Fire protection services include suppression, dispatching, prevention, and training. Sanitary wastewater services include collection and treatment. Street services depend on construction, maintenance, cleaning, and rule enforcement. In each case there is a set of distinct service components that must be integrated in a coherent system of production to support the delivery of services to end-users.

It is also helpful to distinguish *direct producers*, who deliver services directly to end-users, from *indirect* or *auxiliary producers*, who supply services to direct producers. Patrol officers and firefighters, for example, are direct producers, but they depend on the support of a large number of indirect or auxiliary service producers. Trainers deal directly with other producers, not (ordinarily) with end-users. Dispatchers deal with both, linking end-users with direct producers. Although service delivery is largely in the hands of direct producers, it depends on the prior production of auxiliary or support services in the same way that product assembly depends on the prior production of component parts. The effectiveness of service delivery, like the quality of a product, depends on component services that are well designed to fit with other components, requiring some level of coordination across component producers.

Yet each service-component presents a distinct production problem. For each component producers use different inputs and combine them in different ways to yield an output. The factors of production may have to be combined in different proportions for each component. The "recipe" for producing a good patrol service is different from the recipe for producing a good dispatch service or a good investigation service. In particular, service components often vary widely in their requirements for inputs of labor and capital. Some, like a patrol service, are labor intensive; others, like dispatching, are more capital intensive. This results in significant variation in "economies of scale." Nearly all production tasks exhibit increasing returns to scale (a decreasing average cost of production as the scale of production increases) up to a point, but this point varies from one task to another. In general, capital-intensive service components tend to benefit from a larger scale of production than do labor-intensive service components.

Improving efficiency in service production depends on capturing economies of scale while holding down management and coordination costs. A more efficient service sector is one able to draw on larger scales of organization to produce more capital-intensive components but is not constrained to produce more labor-intensive components on the same large scale. This allows the sector to minimize many of the difficulties associated with large-size organizations (measured by the number of employees). Such difficulties include communication distortions, information asymmetries, and the transaction costs of managing production in a large hierarchical structure. Consequently, the more efficient service sectors are likely to be those that utilize a mix of small-scale and large-scale agencies to produce various service components.

FOUR SERVICE SECTORS IN TWO METRO AREAS

The capacity to vary the scale of production, including the scale of production management, is critical to efficient operation within any service sector. The ability to do this, however, is more characteristic of metropolitan areas outside central cities, a proposition confirmed by studies of two metro areas—St. Louis City and County, Missouri, and Allegheny County, Pennsylvania (including Pittsburgh).[1] What is more, the *structure* of each sector closely parallels the structure of the others and follows a pattern consistent with expected economies of scale. At the same time, each sector maintains high levels of interagency coordination, needed to make specialized service-component production work.

The "structure" of a sector has both vertical and horizontal dimensions:

- The *vertical* dimension is concerned with the number of service components separately produced, that is, produced by separately managed organizations with no hierarchical relationship between them. The greater the number of service components separately produced, the greater the "vertical differentiation" of the sector. The fewer the number, the greater the sector's "vertical integration."
- The *horizontal* dimension measures the number of separate producers supplying the same service component in the metro area. The greater this number, the greater the "horizontal differentiation" of production for a specific component. (This dimension is close to what many observers would call service "fragmentation.") The smaller this number, the greater the "horizontal integration" of service production (what many observers would call service "consolidation").

Neither differentiation (fragmentation) nor integration (consolidation) should be considered *inherently* good or bad. Rather, the appropriate degree of differentiation or integration depends on the number of separable service components and the nature of the production process in each case. Both metro areas combine substantial vertical differentiation with a mixture of horizontal integration and differentiation, varying between service components. How this works out in the four service sectors depends on the characteristics of each service.

Parks and Oakerson, commissioned by the ACIR to study two of the most highly fragmented metropolitan areas, examined the organization of police, fire protection, streets, and schools with a focus on the structure of each service sector. This chapter draws mainly on their joint findings and conclusions.[2]

Police Services

The structure of the police service sector in each metro area was analyzed in terms of five service components: (1) patrol, (2) dispatch, (3) investigations, (4) forensics or crime lab, and (5) entry-level training. The results are shown in table 4.1. The structural similarity between the two areas is clear. Both combine a relatively large number of patrol producers with a reduced number of dispatch producers and the highly integrated production of specialized investigations, forensics, and training. The pattern is one that

Table 4.1
Police Service Sectors: Production Units by Service Components,
St. Louis City and County and Allegheny County

Service Component	Number of Production Units	
	St. Louis	Allegheny
Entry-level training	1	2
Forensics	1	2
Major-case investigation	1	2
Dispatch	30	53
Patrol	66	122
Potential producers	92	131

Source: Roger B. Parks and Ronald J. Oakerson, "Comparative Metropolitan
Organization," *Publius* 23, no. 1 (winter 1993): 25.

closely parallels expected economies of scale. Patrol is labor-intensive and the least open to economies of scale of the five service components. Dispatch is somewhat more capital intensive. Plus, it is possible for a single dispatch officer to serve a number of patrol officers. Investigations draws on specialized expertise and skill, expertise that would go unused most of the time if each small patrol producer also attempted to maintain an investigations unit—this due to the lower incidence of serious crime. Forensics requires both expertise and specialized equipment and is able to serve a number of small police-patrol areas. Training is also a specialized activity and one that can serve a large number of departments at the same time.

Note that the number of patrol producers, while greater than for any other service component, is lower than the number of *potential* patrol producers, measured by the number of local governments authorized to operate a police department. In St. Louis County, only 65 out of 91 local governments chose to organize their own police force. In Allegheny County, the ratio is higher—122 out of 131. Especially in the St. Louis case, counting the number of local governments is a poor indicator of police organization even on the patrol component. Most of the nonproducers do provide for police patrol, but they do so by contracting with another municipality or with the county police. The search for economies of scale is relevant even for patrol service, but it results in a larger number of producers (than for the other components) due to the lower threshold (apparently a municipal population of 1–2,000 people)[3] needed to achieve an efficient scale of production.

Dispatch responds to different scale considerations. The ratio of capital to labor expenditure is higher, and a single dispatcher on duty can serve a number of patrol cars, thus increasing the population threshold at which scale economies are realized. The result is a much smaller number of dispatch producers than patrol producers in both metro areas. The exact mode of organization for dispatch varies. Some municipal police departments contract with a nearby department or with an overlying producer, such as county police, for dispatch service. In other cases a cluster of small municipalities jointly organizes and operates a dispatch center. In Allegheny County the joint production of dispatch is sometimes organized through regional Councils of Governments (COGs) composed of municipalities.

The organization of investigations and forensics reflect still different economies of scale. The infrequent occurrence of serious crime cannot justify a large investment in an investigations unit by small police departments or in the technology and specialized personnel required to operate a forensics unit. In the St. Louis area a Major Case Squad handles the investigation of serious crimes throughout the metropolitan area. This investigations unit is composed of officers on assignment from their home departments in both St. Louis City and County as well as from departments in neighboring counties in Missouri and Illinois. County police perform a similar role in Allegheny County outside Pittsburgh. Throughout the United States forensic services are produced only by relatively large city and county agencies, supplemented by state and federal labs.

Training also is organized to realize economies of scale, leading to the establishment of a single training academy to serve both St. Louis City and County and one training academy for Allegheny County outside Pittsburgh. A common entry-level training experience focused on the metropolitan area also facilitates cooperation among separate patrol producers—a consideration that points out the advantage of a local training academy as opposed to one operated at a still larger scale by, perhaps, state police.

Elinor Ostrom, Roger B. Parks, and Gordon Whitaker[4] found patterns of police organization similar to St. Louis and Allegheny Counties in metropolitan areas throughout the United States. Small and medium-size police departments tend to be patrol specialists, placing a greater percentage of their sworn officers on the street than do larger departments. Indirect or auxiliary services tend to be produced by larger units and coordinated in a variety of ways with the production of direct services by smaller units. The degree of integration differs among the components of police service in predictable ways. The result is a metropolitan system of police service production, one that emerges from the independent choices of a variety of provision and production units.

Table 4.2
Public Education Service Sectors: Production Units by Service Components,
St. Louis City and County and Allegheny County

Service Component	Number of Production Units	
	St. Louis	Allegheny
Purchasing, audiovisual, data processing, and special education	2	2
Vocational education	2	6
Regular instruction	24	43

Source: Roger B. Parks and Ronald J. Oakerson, "Comparative Metropolitan
Organization," *Publius* 23, no. 1 (winter 1993): 25.

Public Education

The production of instructional services by public schools was analyzed in
terms of four components: (1) regular instruction, (2) special education,
(3) vocational instruction, and (4) instructional support, including audiovisual materials, data processing, and purchasing. The first three components
are direct services to end-users—students. The last encompassed a broad
range of support services supplied mostly to teachers or, in some cases, school
administrators. In both metro areas each school district produces most of its
own regular instruction, hiring its own teachers and managing its own class-
rooms and schools, but the production of the other components is much more
highly integrated through a small number of producers, as shown in table 4.2.

Specialized instruction, such as instruction for students with disabilities
and vocational-technical instruction, exhibits scale economies not found in
regular instruction for two main reasons: (1) specialized instruction often
requires particular expertise either in subject-matter or teaching methods
and (2) the student clientele is only a fraction of the total student population. The combination of these two characteristics—the employment of
specialized skills relevant only to a minority of students—creates distinctive scale economies. A small school district with sufficient scale to produce
regular instruction may have insufficient scale to produce special education
or vocational training because teachers with the required skills would
have too few students to teach on a full-time basis. Over the past decade or
so "alternative education" has emerged as another specialized mode of
instruction intended for students who are behaviorally unable to cope with
a regular classroom, especially in high school.

In both St. Louis and Allegheny Counties, not unlike most of the United States, special education and vocational training are sorted out from regular instruction and produced, at least in part, by separate agencies. In Allegheny County, school districts cooperate to create "jointures," joint production units that operate vocational-technical schools, sometimes including alternative education programs. Special education in both counties, as well as vocational-technical education in St. Louis, is produced by separately organized, overlay agencies.

The overlay agency in St. Louis County is a countywide Special Education District, an independent special district that functions as both a provision unit and a production unit. Countywide provision clearly facilitates and encourages the organization of production on a countywide basis. However, production is often jointly managed between local school districts and the special district, with the specialized producer supplying teachers and the local district supplying classroom space. This is an arrangement that allows special education to be integrated into the regular instructional program. The same sort of arrangement is found in Allegheny County outside Pittsburgh, where the overlay agency is the Allegheny Intermediate Unit (AIU), an agency created by state law but governed by member school districts. Unlike the Special Education District, intermediate units were created throughout Pennsylvania as a middle tier of school organization—intermediate between local districts and state government. The AIU places special-education teachers in regular schools, conducts special-education programs in schools provided though jointures, and operates one special-education school of its own. Local district participation is at its discretion, and some districts choose to conduct all or part of their own programs.

Instructional support services are also produced by the AIU in Allegheny County, including a wide array of specialized materials and curricular assistance. The AIU often acts as an umbrella agency for organizing more limited consortia among participating districts. In St. Louis County local districts to carry out many of the same activities have created a voluntary agency: Cooperating School Districts of the Suburban St. Louis Area (CSD). Cooperative purchasing, an audiovisual library, data processing, and a countywide music festival are among its services. More recently, area schools also created the Regional Consortium for Education and Technology, which focuses on computer applications.

The principal difference between the two metropolitan counties in the public education sector is the origin and status of overlay agencies. St. Louis County built its overlay agencies from the bottom up, creating both the Special Education District and the CSD at local initiative and discretion. The AIU, in contrast, was created at state initiative and discretion. Local district membership in the AIU is mandatory, and the AIU has a funding stream that is in part independent of local district decisions. The two counties therefore represent two different models of service sector development. Both lead to vertical differentiation. However, both overlay agencies in St. Louis County resulted from specific local efforts to secure perceived economies of scale. The AIU, which was created on the basis of decisions made outside of Allegheny County, presumes the existence of broad economies of scale that require an overlay agency. One model is based on responses to specific local initiatives, while the other model attempts to anticipate local needs.

Streets

The basic distinction to be made among street-service components is between a set of services associated with planning, construction, and improvement, on the one hand, and another set of services associated with maintenance, on the other hand. However, the ACIR studies focused mostly on maintenance services, first distinguishing arterial surface maintenance from residential surface maintenance and then further sorting out purchasing (a support service) and sweeping (another direct service). Street services in fact exhibit much greater diversity among components delivered directly to the end-users of streets. A more inclusive study would examine street lighting and snow plowing as separate components. Surface maintenance can also be disaggregated into multiple activities, distinguishing, for example, preventive maintenance such as crack sealing from repairs such as filling potholes.

The diversity of street service components leads to a high degree of vertical differentiation—many different producers, often private, of many different components. A large portion of street services, however, is highly integrated in both metro areas. This is the production of services on arterial streets, which is divided between county and state agencies. With the exception of a few service-components, these agencies produce a full range of maintenance services for the arterial streets provided through county and state governments. On the other end of the spectrum, there are a very large number of *potential* producers of residential street services. In St. Louis County this number is greatly magnified by the presence of more than 400 private street associations, organized subdivisions or RCAs that own and therefore provide for their own streets.

As in the case of police services, however, the number of providers is a poor guide to the number of service producers. Only one or two RCAs were found that organized their own service production to any extent—one large RCA had a single employee and another very small RCA organized street repair through neighborhood volunteers. Surface maintenance and repair was almost entirely contracted out to private producers (no count of private producers was attempted). Sweeping was often contracted out to an overlying municipality. Among small municipalities (those with fewer than 1,000 residents), only one out of ten responding to a survey reported producing any street maintenance services in-house; the remainder contracted privately. Out of a total of 520 providers of street services (including 93 governmental units), only 77 provision units were engaged in the production of residential street maintenance.

In Allegheny County the production of residential street maintenance was divided between municipalities and groups of municipalities organized as COGs. All but a single municipality maintained its own street or public works department. Sweeping, however, was frequently produced under contract by a COG. One COG had organized a joint public works team among five small and financially stressed municipalities, pooling personnel, equipment, and materials to produce crack sealing. Still another COG operated a joint purchasing program for street materials and equipment, available to any municipality in the county. In St. Louis County, the county chapter of

Table 4.3
Street Service Sectors: Production Units by Service Components, St. Louis City and County and Allegheny County

Service Component	Number of Production Units*	
	St. Louis	Allegheny
Arterial street maintenance	3	3
Purchasing	58	70
Street sweeping	77	~ 25
Residential street maintenance	77	125
Government providers	91	130
Private providers	427	0

*Includes only government producers, not private producers active in residential street maintenance, especially in St. Louis.

Source: Roger B. Parks and Ronald J. Oakerson, "Comparative Metropolitan Organization," *Publius* 23, no. 1 (winter 1993): 25.

the American Public Works Association had begun a similar program, picking up some nineteen participants.

Patterns in street service production are somewhat less clear than in the other services. There appear to be greater economies of scale in sweeping than in the performance of some of the other maintenance routines—this emerges most clearly from the pattern of production in Allegheny County. However, St. Louis County patterns indicate economies of scale in virtually all residential street components. The presence of a large number of small private providers (RCAs plus some very small municipalities) in St. Louis County contributes to the variation in production patterns between the two counties—more contracting-out in St. Louis County with the exception of sweeping in Allegheny County. Consistent across both counties, however, is the high degree of integration in arterial street services accompanied by much greater differentiation in residential street services, as shown in table 4.3.

Fire Protection

St. Louis and Allegheny Counties have developed quite different approaches to the *provision* of fire protection, which carries over into substantially different patterns of production. Allegheny County continues to rely heavily on volunteers, while St. Louis County utilizes mostly full-time, professional firefighters. In table 4.4, volunteer fire companies are treated as production units. Actually, provision tends to be shared between municipalities and the volunteer organizations. Some municipalities own the fire station, employ a full-time driver, or contribute equipment. In total there are some 250 volunteer fire companies in the county, drawing on approximately 20,000 volunteers to produce fire, rescue, and emergency medical services.

As a result, Allegheny County has a much larger number of producers than St. Louis County. In fact, the number of fire-protection producers in Allegheny County exceeds the number of municipalities, while in St. Louis County the number of fire-protection producers is considerably less than the number of municipalities. Numerous Allegheny municipalities are served by more than one volunteer company, while small St. Louis municipalities (as well as unincorporated areas) are generally served by an overlying fire protection district, which usually functions as both provision unit and production unit. Just over half of the producers in the county are fire protection districts.

Economies of scale appear to dictate different production arrangements when there are full-time firefighters. Volunteers are part-timers. By drawing on volunteers, producers eliminate not only the out-of-pocket cost of labor,

Table 4.4
Fire Protection Service Sectors: Production Units by Service
Components, St. Louis City and County and Allegheny County

Service Component	Number of Production Units	
	St. Louis	Allegheny
Entry-level training	2	2
Dispatch	20	40
Fire suppression	43	~253
Formal provision units	116	13

Source: Roger B. Parks and Ronald J. Oakerson, "Comparative Metropolitan
Organization," *Publius* 23, no. 1 (winter 1993): 25.

but also the downtime experienced by full-time firefighters. Even if volunteers were paid by the hour, they would be cheaper than full-timers. From the standpoint of an efficient allocation of resources, volunteers are arguably more efficient. When volunteers are used, the real labor cost (as opposed to out-of-pocket cost) is limited to the actual time used to fight fires or perform other needed tasks. This eliminates any problem of excess capacity with respect to personnel. No matter how small the fire station, no one is standing around waiting for fires to fight. As a result, the production efficiency of relatively small fire stations is enhanced by the use of volunteers. Conversely, the efficiency of small fire stations is reduced in the presence of full-time firefighters, explaining the reliance on a smaller number of larger producers in St. Louis County.

The ACIR studies distinguished three major components of fire-related service production: entry-level training, communications/dispatch, and fire suppression. Apart from the striking differences at the structural base of the sector, the pattern across the three components is consistent for the two counties. Fire suppression is consistently more highly differentiated, while communications/dispatch is much less differentiated, and training is highly integrated. The pattern closely resembles that observed for police services.

COORDINATION AND MUTUAL AID

Specialized production by separate agencies depends on interagency coordination to make it work. Coordination occurs on both the vertical and horizontal dimensions of a service sector. Producers of different service components coordinate vertically, as when a dispatcher from one agency dispatches an officer from another agency. Different producers of the same service component, especially those who deliver services directly to end-users, coordinate horizontally, often by assisting one another in the field. In a differentiated service sector, coordination and mutual aid are based on mutual self-interest among autonomous agencies rather than on central direction.

The amount of coordination and mutual aid occurring on a voluntary basis is often surprising to many observers, although the amount varies among service sectors. Mutual aid is particularly common among police-patrol and fire-suppression producers, but less frequent among street-maintenance producers—differences that can be explained by the nature of the production process in each case. In the public schools, coordination between producers of regular instruction and producers of special education goes beyond mutual aid to include the coordinated delivery of similar services to the same students. High levels of coordination are also found among the producers of library services, social services, and recreation services.

Mutual aid is used to solve two important production problems: (1) problems that physically cross jurisdictional boundaries, such as fleeing felons, and (2) peak-load problems, the circumstance created by occasional extreme demands on service capacity, such as a large fire that exceeds the capacity of any single fire station. Only the very largest police and fire departments in the nation can handle peak-loads without outside assistance. St. Louis County fire-protection producers have also created first-response agreements designed to allow the closest fire station to respond to a fire whether or not the fire is located in that station's jurisdiction. In this way local-government boundaries do not interfere with getting a fire truck to the scene as quickly as possible. Mutual aid among street-service producers, by contrast, is limited mostly to equipment sharing, which is yet another way to capture economies of scale. Peak-loads in street services tend to be seasonal and to occur at the same time for all producers. This restricts the potential for mutual aid. However, there tends to be considerable coordination in planning and improvements between county and state producers of arterial street services.[5]

In addition to mutual aid, coordination among direct service producers also occurs by means of "alternation," dividing up production responsibility on the basis of time, space, or clientele.[6] In this way producers with overlapping service responsibilities can avoid duplication. The overlap in jurisdictions of county and municipal police departments in St. Louis County, for example, does not usually lead to duplicative patrol patterns. Instead, the two departments alternate in time or otherwise divide their shared responsibilities. Police alternation is a common pattern throughout the U.S.[7]

Both formal and informal arrangements are used to support coordination. Frequently, mutual aid pacts are signed as formal intergovernmental agreements. Even in their absence, however, assistance is usually rendered when requested. The driving force behind coordination is self-interested reciprocity, which often can operate without a legally binding agreement. Presumably, agencies that refuse to cooperate with others will be unable to depend on others when the need arises.

AN INDUSTRIAL ORGANIZATION MODEL

The organization of public service sectors strongly resembles the organization of private industries. Each service sector is akin to a differentiated industry, one composed of multiple firms of various sizes instead of a single giant company. The economic theory of industrial organization is more relevant to the study of service sectors than the standard theory of public administration, which tends to presume a hierarchical model of organization.[8] Like industries, service sectors are organized through arrangements that emerge among relatively autonomous producers. The base of a public service industry consists of agencies that deliver services directly to end-users. Other producers are added as needed to realize economies of scale, either by contracting with an existing agency or by adding an organizational overlay (joint production unit or special-purpose district). Each producer has considerable independence from the others, yet the sector exhibits a high degree of coordination, motivated by mutual self-interest.

An alternative way to organize service production is through a dominant public bureaucracy, such as that found in most large central cities. This mode of organization is analogous to an industry in which production is concentrated in a single large firm. The scale of the bureaucracy, measured by the size of the population served, usually equals or exceeds the size threshold needed to produce service components that require relatively large-scale production. The production of various service components can then be carried out by subunits of the bureaucracy. Components that benefit from lower size thresholds can be organized into multiple subunits (as when police patrols operate from precinct stations). Each subunit is accountable to hierarchical superiors; instructions and communications are subject to central direction. Although some service components may be contracted out, contracting decisions are made centrally, and contractors are accountable to central management. The differentiation of production, whether within or outside the bureaucracy, is thus subordinated to central control.

Because both a partially differentiated service sector and a fully integrated public bureaucracy are able to capture economies of scale, a comparative assessment of the two modes of organization turns on the issue of coordination. As discussed above, coordination has benefits; however, it is also costly to participants, and coordination costs limit the amount of coordination that occurs, whether within a single organization or between different organizations. Coordination costs are transaction costs, which vary with the time and effort needed for reaching agreements, resolving conflicts, and, more generally, getting along with others. Costs as well as benefits help to determine the amount of coordination that occurs in any setting.

The structure of a service sector represents a trade-off between the costs of coordinating *within* agencies and the costs of coordinating *between* agencies. Both intra-agency coordination and interagency coordination have limits. The objective of hierarchical organization within agencies is to economize on transaction costs by mandating coordination.[9] Interagency coordination, by contrast, is voluntary and, therefore, subject to negotiation. This leads easily—too easily—to the conclusion that coordination between agencies is more costly—a conclusion that must be sharply qualified. Coordination costs increase with the number of people who must be included in a decision. As hierarchical organizations increase in size, the coordination costs within those organizations also tend to increase.[10] Bureaucracy, by mandating coordination, tends to widen its scope beyond the parties immediately concerned.[11] Theoretically, at some point in the expansion of a bureaucracy, intra-agency coordination costs begin to exceed interagency coordination costs for some activities. For example, neighboring police departments can agree to coordinate their actions without consulting anyone outside their communities, while adjacent police precincts in a large city bureaucracy may have to secure the agreement of hierarchical superiors before they can agree to coordinate. There is also a possibility that large-scale bureaucracies may introduce too much coordination, or coordination that is not beneficial, by requiring approval for decisions that subunits are capable of making on their own.

Separate agencies are often thought to "proliferate" in fragmented metropolitan areas. The extent of differentiation within service sectors, however, is limited by interagency coordination costs. Producers of direct services that find it more advantageous to produce an indirect service component in-house can be expected to do so. Agencies are added only as needed to capture economies of scale.

Both integration—bringing activities within a single agency—and differentiation—dividing activities among different agencies—have limited utility. It is possible *both* for a single agency to grow too large and for a service sector to develop too many agencies. In general, a metropolitan service sector that is partially differentiated is likely to exhibit lower coordination costs and therefore *higher levels of beneficial coordination* than a fully integrated public bureaucracy. As a result, so-called "fragmented" metropolitan areas, which maintain a multiplicity of producers, have a greater potential for effective coordination in the production of services than fully consolidated metropolitan government, which integrates the production of services across the board.

In principle, there is nothing to prevent a large central city from differentiating the organization of production by contracting out selected service components to a number of small-scale agencies. The structure of the provision side of a local public economy, however, appears to affect the structure of the production side. Empirically, a metropolitan area "fragmented" on the provision side is much more likely than a consolidated metropolitan government to develop highly differentiated service sectors on the production side. Yet small and large municipal governments share one characteristic in common: the tendency to produce most direct services in-house. Only the smallest municipalities—pure provision units—contract out for production tasks like police patrol. Large cities often contract out for the production of selected support services, but, despite high coordination costs, they seldom contract out for the delivery of services directly to end-users. Thus, for example, virtually all large city governments maintain large police departments that produce patrol in-house.

One reason for the lack of service-sector differentiation in large central cities may be the lack of available contractors. When large cities do contract with small units to deliver direct services, it is usually in the social-service sector, where a relatively large number of private voluntary organizations exist as potential contractors. Small municipalities can draw on both larger overlying units—counties and special districts—and adjacent units as contractors. Production capacity is distributed among multiple producers, each a potential competitor for the other. The development of neighborhood governments in large cities would not only create new provision units but would also create potential contractors for direct services that continue to be provided by city governments. This could lead to more differentiated service sectors within large central cities.

EVALUATING SERVICE SECTORS

Service sectors in St. Louis and Allegheny Counties exhibit strong structural similarities—similarities both across four different sectors and across the two metropolitan counties. The pattern is, in general, one that combines the highly differentiated delivery of direct service to end-users with the more integrated production of various support services. The degree of service integration varies with expected economies of scale. Some service components, such as police and fire dispatch, are only moderately integrated, while others, such as training and criminal investigations, are concentrated in one or two agencies.

The pattern is one that makes considerable economic sense. By joining a few large-scale agencies to many small-scale agencies, service sectors simultaneously gain the benefits of both large and small-scale organization. At the same time, a high level of coordination among multiple service producers indicates that interagency coordination costs are relatively low. Structural similarities consistent with economies of scale together with high levels of interagency coordination suggest strong tendencies toward efficiency in service production.

Within each service sector, however, there is substantial variation in agency size, especially among direct service producers such as municipal police departments. In St. Louis County, for example, municipal police departments ranged in size from four to seventy-seven full-time officers.[12] The existence of such variety is due to some mixture of three factors: (1) variation in demand (including both willingness and ability to pay),[13] (2) size ranges over which there are constant returns to scale, and (3) remaining, uncaptured scale economies. By controlling for indicators of service demand and comparing the per capita expenditures of various size departments, it is statistically possible to estimate the magnitude of uncaptured scale economies within the structure of a service sector. For St. Louis County police services, the magnitude of uncaptured scale economies was estimated at 50 to 70 cents per capita for each 1,000 residents.[14] In Allegheny County this amount was only 5 cents per capita—not statistically significant from zero.[15]

The most direct evidence for the benefits of production structures like those found in St. Louis and Allegheny Counties comes from a 1985 study of police services by Roger B. Parks,[16] utilizing data from seventy-six metropolitan areas. Parks focused on the relative technical efficiency with which police departments in each metropolitan area transform resource-inputs into two outputs: (1) number of officers on the streets and (2) number of reported crimes cleared by arrest. Service sectors were measured along two structural dimensions: (1) relative agency dominance in (a) homicide investigation and (b) radio-communications (dispatch) and (2) the multiplicity and autonomy of policy patrol producers. His analysis found the *highest technical efficiency* in metropolitan areas that exhibited *high relative dominance* in both homicide investigation and radio communications combined with *high multiplicity and autonomy* of patrol producers. These are service sectors with the same basic structure as those found in St. Louis and Allegheny Counties. By the same token, he found the *lowest technical efficiency* in metropolitan areas characterized by *low relative dominance* in homicide investigation and radio communications combined with *low multiplicity and autonomy* of patrol producers. These are service sectors that have less vertical differentiation, that is, less differentiation among the producers of different service components having different economies of scale; at the same time, they have less horizontal differentiation in patrol and more horizontal differentiation in the production of key support services. A few midsize to large departments, each attempting to produce the full range of service components in-house, would fit the picture.

In addition to the similarities across sectors, there are some striking variations. Variations across the four service sectors derive from differences in the nature of the service-mix being produced, such as the greater variety in the complement of direct services associated with street maintenance. These variations are, in fact, consistent with the observed similarities. That is, both the similarities and the differences derive from the same source: the nature of the good or service being produced.

Variations across the two metropolitan counties within the same sector tell a somewhat different story, inasmuch as they derive from the sometimes widely divergent organization of the provision side—especially, the use of volunteer fire companies in Allegheny County and private street associations in St. Louis County. The latter differences are associated with longstanding community traditions—different forms of social capital, peculiar to each metropolitan area.[17] Each county has developed a distinctive institutional style of social capital formation, affecting the structure of relevant service sectors. Social capital formation is probably much more difficult than service production to replicate from one area to another. A recommended use of volunteer fire departments in St. Louis County, for example, would presume a form of social capital that does not exist. The same could be said for private street maintenance in Allegheny County. The history of social capital formation thus seems to limit the feasible degree of institutional transfer among metropolitan areas.

CONCLUSION

The large number of police departments, fire departments, street departments, school districts, and other independent production units typically found in metropolitan areas outside central cities is a common focus of critical comment. Critics presume that service production in this context (1) fails to capture economies of scale and (2) lacks coordination in the delivery of services to citizens. Both presumptions are unwarranted: first, because service components that benefit from the economies of large-scale organization tend to be highly integrated in one or two agencies; second, because independent service producers normally coordinate their activities extensively. By failing to examine the organization of service sectors, critics of "fragmentation" both overstate the benefits of further service consolidation and understate its costs.

What matters is not simply the number of municipal departments that share in the production of any given service, but rather the structure of the entire service sector. An optimal structure is one that *combines service integration and differentiation* so that multiple agencies can capture economies of scale while economizing on coordination costs.

Service sectors differ across service-types. Police sectors, fire protection sectors, and public education sectors all present a somewhat different organizational configuration that depends on the variable nature of the production process. Within each sector, the number of producers varies among distinct service-components. Components with substantial economies of scale have fewer producers; components with lesser economies of scale have more producers. Tying together the separate producers within each sector is a pervasive pattern of interagency coordination.

The critics of metropolitan fragmentation usually recommend, at a minimum, extensive service consolidation beyond that which already exists. Although it is virtually certain that some structural adjustment could be made in any metropolitan area that would increase production efficiency, locating these potential adjustments is not easy—especially for external observers such as most professional consultants on metropolitan reorganization. Adjustments that increase efficiency depend on rather complex trade-offs that take into account both interagency and intra-agency coordination costs as well as expected economies of scale. Wholesale consolidations frequently do not result in demonstrable cost savings.[18] This is probably due to the fact that most potential economies of scale have already been captured through vertical differentiation and interagency coordination. In other words, so much cooperation is already occurring that full service consolidation has little more to offer. Too much consolidation can even make matters worse by moving coordination completely inside large public bureaucracies and thereby increasing coordination costs.

In static economic-efficiency terms no metropolitan area can be said to "have arrived" at an efficiency optimum, taking all factors into account. Local public economies are far too complex to permit such perfection, and even if it did exist, it would not last for long due to continuous changes in many of the relevant parameters. In dynamic terms, however, what counts the most is the direction in which the local public economy is moving. An area that adapts to changing conditions by moving toward efficiency is preferable to one that sits on a solution that was efficient, or thought to be so, decades before. Studies of key service sectors in two of the nation's most highly fragmented metropolitan areas strongly suggest the existence of an *efficiency dynamic*—local public economies in which there is a continuous or recurring search for more efficient organizational combinations. Accounting for and sustaining such a dynamic, not to mention creating one where it does not now exist, goes beyond provision and production structures, however, and into the subject of the next chapter: governance.

5

METROPOLITAN GOVERNANCE — WITHOUT METROPOLITAN GOVERNMENT

INTRODUCTION

The standard prescription of metropolitan reform is to create metropolitan governments, consolidating both provision and production responsibilities in a single areawide unit of government. Although—with only a few, partial exceptions—efforts to create metro-governments have not met with success, the ideal of a single government for a metropolitan area retains a powerful hold on reformers, who fear that a multiplicity of local governments necessarily leads to the "balkanization" of the metropolis. No doubt, absent any workable structure of governance, metropolitan problems would largely go unattended and conflicts would be exacerbated rather than resolved. Governmental relationships in such a metro-area would indeed be dominated by conflict with little hope of constructive resolution.

Governance is concerned with making and enforcing rules, a process distinguishable from providing and producing services. Local public economies require an ability to make and enforce rules that apply to multiple provision and production units on an areawide basis. Rule making can be organized separately from service provision, however, just as provision can be organized separately from production. This implies that a metropolitan government is not a necessary condition of metropolitan governance. The necessary condition—an areawide capacity for rule making—can be achieved without creating a metro-wide unit of government able to dominate the provision-side of the local public economy. This chapter explores the means of doing so—of achieving metropolitan governance without metropolitan government.

In general, metro-governance in a fragmented metropolis has three central features:

1. Substantial governing authority is assigned to local citizens, allowing citizens to make the basic decisions that shape the structure of the provision side of the local public economy.
2. A metropolitan civil society emerges to identify problems, negotiate differences, and arrange settlements that serve as the basis for areawide rules and collective action.
3. An overlying jurisdiction—usually state government—is available to translate areawide decisions into enforceable rules that apply uniquely to the metro-area.

LOCAL-GOVERNMENT CONSTITUTIONS

Local public economies in the U.S. are equipped with what amounts to a local-government "constitution," a set of rules used to constitute the provision side and determine the authority that can be exercised by its various units. The term "constitution" is used here in a functional rather than nominal sense. Most of the relevant rules are found either in state constitutions or (mostly) in state statutes. Although public economies, like private economies, vary in the degree to which they are regulated by law, the basic rules of the local public economy are analogous to property rights, establishing a general framework of authority within the economy functions.[1] Of central importance is the authority to create, modify, and dissolve provision units. The structure of the provision side—including the number and variety of provision units—depends on who can exercise this authority and under what conditions.

Local-government constitutions depend on two levels of choice: (1) an *enabling* level that determines a set of rules that local citizens can use to create and modify local governments and (2) a *chartering* level that determines the specific charter of a unit of local government when citizens act to bring it into existence in accordance with enabling rules. The enabling rules can be sorted into four types:

1. *Rules of association*—those that establish processes, such as municipal incorporation, that enable local citizens to create municipalities or other units endowed with certain governmental powers.
2. *Boundary adjustment rules*—to enable local citizens and officials to alter the boundaries of existing units.
3. *Fiscal rules*—those that determine the revenue-raising authority of various local units; and
4. *Contracting rules*—to enable local units to enter into a variety of mutually agreeable relationships with one another and with private firms.[2]

One of the basic issues pertaining to local government constitutions is the distribution of authority between the "enabling" level and the "chartering" level. The term "home rule" is traditionally applied to local government arrangements that reserve substantial authority to the chartering level. The ability of local residents to frame their own charter when choosing to constitute a local government unit is fundamental to home rule,[3] but the degree to which states permit an autonomous determination of the powers of local government by local citizens varies widely.[4] Of special interest, usually, is the issue of *fiscal* home rule, namely, the degree to which local taxing authority is derived from local charters rather than state law. Some state restrictions on local officials, however, constitute an empowerment of local citizens, such as those requiring citizen consent to tax-rate increases in local referenda. Home rule is most commonly applied to municipalities (often of a minimum size), less frequently to counties and townships, and seldom to special districts. The latter, when created by citizens, may exercise only those powers defined as a matter of state law.[5]

A typical "constitution" for a local public economy allocates chartering authority as follows:

- *An initial set of local government units exists by default.* As provided by the constitution or laws of the state, usually a county or a township (or some combination of the two) functions as the primary unit of local government unless citizens choose to create additional units.

- *Local citizens may create new units of government by following initiative and referendum procedures.* Some units have minimum size requirements in terms of population or area. The initiative petition specifies the boundaries of the proposed unit. When approved by popular vote in a referendum (either by a simple majority or an extraordinary majority), a new unit of government has been created. Enabling rules present citizens with a menu of possibilities—a set of optional local governments. Citizens usually may choose to create a municipality (where one does not already exist) and various special-purpose districts. The authority of the unit being created is limited by the enabling rule.

- *Enlarging the boundaries of an existing unit of government requires the consent of the community being annexed.* This usually depends on a popular referendum. Often, concurrent majorities are required in both the annexing and annexed areas.

- *The consolidation of two or more local government units requires approval by concurrent majorities voting in separate referenda.* This rule was endorsed by the ACIR in 1982.[6] A single referendum could allow a larger unit to decide unilaterally to absorb a smaller community.

- *Citizens may also choose to dissolve an optional unit of government by means of initiative and referendum.* When an optional unit is dissolved, local government reverts to the default unit provided by state law.

A large number of variations exist on this general theme—sometimes constraining the authority of citizens, sometimes enlarging it. One constraint is the limited variety of special-purpose districts that citizens may create. States vary considerably in how large a menu they offer citizens. There are also variations in "nesting" rules—specifically, whether a new unit is nested within an existing unit or displaces it. In New York State, for example, villages are nested within townships, but cities displace townships. In Pennsylvania, both cities and boroughs (the equivalent of a village) displace townships, and organizing a city or borough can become an act of secession. Sometimes annexation requires the consent of the default unit partially losing jurisdiction. This was the case in St. Louis County, Missouri, when for many years state court rulings in effect gave county government a veto over municipal annexation. The county's incentive to veto annexations was closely tied to its operating as a de facto municipality—providing and producing a wide range of services—within a large unincorporated area.[7]

The *full configuration* of enabling rules—not simply the rules for each type of local unit taken separately—affects the pattern of provision and production units that citizens and officials choose to establish.[8] For example, as discussed in chapter 3, the creation of special districts in some states may derive in part from restrictive tax and debt ceilings imposed by state law on local general-purpose governments. If such rules lead, perversely, to a greater number of special districts than citizens would otherwise choose to create, the effect is inefficient. This result, however, is a consequence of the fiscal rules that pertain to general-purpose governments, not the rules of association that pertain to the formation of special districts.

Incorporation and annexation rules, to take another example, are closely related. If state law allows unilateral annexation by municipalities, without obtaining separate concurrence from voters in the area to be annexed, this may encourage "defensive" incorporation by communities that otherwise would not choose to incorporate. On the other hand, some communities confronted by a more encompassing incorporation effort may seek annexation by an adjacent municipality as a preferred alternative. Incorporation rules vary (both among states and among types of municipalities within states) from a simple plurality of those voting to extraordinary majorities. A strategy of seeking annexation to avoid incorporation could indicate that the collective decision-rule for incorporation is too permissive, allowing some parts of a proposed municipality to impose unwanted incorporation on other communities within the proposed set of boundaries.

Consolidation rules also vary. For example, in many states consolidation rules vary between municipalities and school districts. While concurrent majorities are required for municipalities, school districts can be reorganized on the basis of a single vote across the proposed district. School district reorganization can also be proposed by state or county officials, rather than initiated by citizen petition. The obvious intent of such rules is to facilitate school district consolidation, which is by far, nationwide, the most successful consolidation movement undertaken to date, reducing the number of districts from more than 100,000 in 1942 to fewer than 15,000 today.

CHOOSING BOUNDARIES

One of the basic governance issues affecting local public economies is the question of who is best suited to determine the boundaries of provision units. Of course, the issue of how large or how small any given unit should be is closely related to the question of how many units there ought to be in a given area. Because boundaries determine who is in and who is out, the choice of boundaries is intimately tied up with identifying a community of interest and matching a community with a jurisdiction. Satisfying the basic criteria of provision, such as preference expression, fiscal equivalence, and accountability (discussed in chapter 1), depends upon having reasonably correct boundaries. But how does one know what is correct? Can the correct boundaries be objectively determined? Or is boundary choice an inherently subjective process of decision making?

One objective factor to be considered in choosing appropriate boundaries is the scale of effects associated with the consumption of a good or service—namely, the spatial or geographical extent of an area directly affected when a good or service is supplied (or not supplied). The scale of effects associated with some goods and services, such as the supply of residential (non-arterial) streets or routine police (or security) patrol, is quite small. Other goods and services, such as arterial streets and police crime solving, have direct effects that are broader in extent, affecting larger communities of interest.

Extent or scale of effects, however, is not a determining factor. At most this criterion can establish the need for a *minimum* size jurisdiction for specific goods and services. If individual households hire a security patrol, for example, neighbors who do not contribute will nevertheless derive a benefit. They can act as "free-riders." Private provision, therefore, cannot fully aggregate demand for this service, but the exact scale on which demand is best aggregated, collectively, remains indeterminate. Boundaries clearly can be too small.[9] On the other hand, boundaries larger than required by this criterion may still be optimal. The upper limit on the appropriate size of a provision unit is much more ambiguous. The determining factors involve the variability of citizen preferences and the way that citizens with similar preferences cluster geographically. At issue is the extent to which a relatively homogeneous good or service, provided at a given level, can satisfy a geographically defined community of interest. Some "neighborhoods," defined as a community with a distinct set of interests and preferences when compared to surrounding communities, may be quite small; others may be much larger.

Fiscal equivalence and accountability may in some circumstances suggest a more circumscribed set of boundaries than suggested by preference homogeneity. A large community with homogeneous preferences may still experience difficulties in maintaining accountability to citizens if the aggregate number of citizens increases beyond some point. The same circumstance may create incentives for some neighborhoods to raid the central treasury at the expense of others, leading to problems with fiscal equivalence. In this way, the criteria of fiscal equivalence and accountability can modify considerations based solely upon homogeneity of preferences.

To make these determinations requires knowledge of the preferences (for goods and services) of individuals in the communities involved. Local citizens, therefore, can best make the trade-offs required between preference satisfaction, on the one hand, and the transaction costs associated with organizing and operating additional provision units, on the other. These costs, as discussed in chapter 1, constrain the degree to which citizens choose to create additional provision units, and include the costs of citizen participation necessary to articulate preferences and secure accountability from officials.

Appropriate boundary determinations (from the standpoint of provision-side efficiency) depend on rules that allow citizens, collectively, to make the needed trade-offs. Without knowing the preferences of individuals for goods and services, as well as the trade-off they would make between preference satisfaction and the transaction costs of operating additional units, there is no fully objective method for determining the optimal size of a provision unit. On this issue, citizens become the experts.

The minimum-size jurisdiction appropriate to organize provision varies substantially among different goods and services. Some types of goods and services can be provided on a "neighborhood" scale. Other types obviously serve a broader community of interest, such as arterial streets, some types of law enforcement (e.g., investigation of major crimes), public transportation, airports, and some types of park and recreation services. This implies that a set of provision units where smaller units are nested—like "Chinese boxes"—inside larger units will tend to be optimal.[10] One cannot determine *a priori* how much "nesting"—how many boxes inside boxes—there ought to be within a particular local area. To decide in advance that a "two-tier" arrangement, for example, is appropriate does not take into account the potential variety in organization on both the provision side and the production side—the diverse scale considerations that apply to service production in addition to the potential diversity of community preferences. The amount of nesting or territorial overlap that is appropriate can vary within, as well as among, local public economies. As with the choice of boundaries, citizens are the preferred decision-makers.

No one can determine the "correct" or "best" pattern of organization for a local public economy *a priori*. This includes organization of both the provision side and the production side. Instead of trying to determine an ideal structure of metropolitan or regional organization, a normative analysis of local public economies should focus on the "rules of the game" in order to help individuals and communities to order their relationships with one another in more productive ways.

Rules governing incorporation, consolidation, and annexation, as well as disincorporation and de-annexation, define the decision-making processes by which boundary determinations are made and altered.[11] Comprehensive reform proposals such as city-county consolidations, which would greatly diminish the number of independent provision units in a metropolitan area, are, however, much more often defeated than accepted by local voters.[12] New units are established with some frequency, and marginal adjustments in the boundaries of existing units are also fairly common. Comprehensive changes that alter a number of boundaries at once, however, are extremely rare.

One cannot explain the existing structure of a local public economy without reference to these "rules of the game." It may seem odd, for example, that relatively homogeneous suburbs generally exhibit a greater number and variety of provision units than more diverse central cities.[13] One explanation lies in the rules used to organize provision units. Suburban growth begins in an unincorporated area, but the rules of incorporation and annexation frequently allow diverse communities to make independent boundary determinations. Most central cities were a product of a much different decision-making process; often their boundaries were determined by state legislatures, or the rules then in place allowed annexation without citizen consent. Also, as discussed in chapter 3, once a city is incorporated, the rules tend to preclude or inhibit the development of smaller, nested provision units—neighborhood governments—within its boundaries.

Beginning in 1961, ACIR began to encourage states to enact rules that limit the number of new incorporations.[14] Eventually, this prescription was broadened to include the establishment of new local governments of all types, including both general-purpose and special-purpose governments, as well as the dissolution of local governments considered to be nonviable. The principal institutional mechanism recommended to achieve this end was a *boundary review agency*, established on either a statewide or local areawide basis. The broad purpose of such an agency is to control incorporations and annexations in order to assure an orderly pattern of service delivery and to promote a better match between fiscal capacity and service needs. The Commission also proposed that the same agency be used to enjoin intergovernmental contracting among local jurisdictions when this practice is seen to split the tax base without compensating advantages.[15]

Ten states, all located in the Midwestern or western United States, established some sort of state or local boundary review agency over a ten-year period beginning in 1959.[16] A 1968 review concluded that all operating boundary review agencies had successfully reduced the "proliferation" of local governments.[17] Neither growth nor reduction in the number of governments, however, provides evidence that any given number is suboptimal. An Illinois study cautions against "universal application of policies, such as boundary commissions, to generally limit or restrict use of single-purpose special districts."[18]

Frequently, the establishment of a new unit is an alternative to expanding the boundaries of an existing unit. If so, officials in existing local governments may desire to constrain incorporations in order to reduce competitive pressures on their own units—pressures that can be efficiency-inducing. Findings from an empirical study of Local Agency Formation Commissions (LAFCOs) in California support this interpretation.[19] Boundary review agencies may come to represent the interests of existing local government officials as opposed to the interests of citizens.

In 1987, therefore, the ACIR modified its approach to the boundary-adjustment issue, recommending that states exercise caution in the creation and use of boundary review agencies having the capability of vetoing incorporations and annexations that are, or would be, approved by local citizens in popular referenda.[20] The new recommendation is consistent with the view, sketched above, that local public economies should emerge in response to citizen choices rather than official design.

CRAFTING LOCAL-GOVERNMENT AUTHORITY

In a highly differentiated (or fragmented) metropolitan area, with some units nested within others, the authority of each governmental unit is apt to carry consequences for others. This suggests that local governmental authority may need to be rather carefully crafted so as to reduce negative spillovers between jurisdictions. Taxing authority is an especially sensitive issue. Sales taxes allow jurisdictions to obtain revenues directly from one another's residents, and property taxes can involve local governments in competition for a limited tax base. The general problem is one of maintaining fiscal equivalence—getting what you pay for and paying for what you get—in a situation in which it is sometimes difficult to tie taxes to benefits or benefits to taxes. Some limited form of tax sharing among jurisdictions in a metropolitan area can alleviate the tensions among them, although arriving at a formula for sharing revenues can be very contentious. St. Louis County, for example, allows municipalities to choose whether to join a sales-tax pool or to keep their sales tax revenues for themselves.[21]

Service provision decisions can also involve interdependencies among local jurisdictions. For example, a municipal decision of whether to provide police service is affected by the availability of a county sheriff as a default option. If many or most municipalities are providing for their own police service, a municipality that chooses to rely on the county sheriff is then securing a one-way subsidy from the rest of the county. One response to this problem is a countywide rule that requires all municipalities to provide police service at some minimum level. Such a rule would not require that each municipality produce its own police service, only that it pay for the service it gets. Production could be arranged through contracting, either with the county sheriff or an adjacent municipality. This particular problem is also one that arose in St. Louis County and was resolved through a state law that requires all municipalities in the county with a population of at least 500 people to *provide* police service on a full-time basis.[22] This rule contributes to the relatively high incidence of interlocal police contracting that occurs in the county.

One reason that St. Louis County can effectively address such problems is the ability of the Missouri legislature to enact what amounts to special local legislation for a metropolitan county. When broad agreement exists among the members of the county's delegation to the legislature (thirty-one representatives and seven senators, all elected from districts), other legislators defer to their preference on so-called local bills. This allows the "local-government constitution" embodied in state law to be tailored to local circumstances. The result is a form of metropolitan governance that includes the ability to adapt the rules governing a local public economy to the unique needs and opportunities found in specific metropolitan areas.

Although many states and metropolitan areas possess such a capability, it is not found everywhere. State constitutional prohibitions of special legislation for specific local governments can preclude state-level efforts to address the unique problems of a metropolitan area. This is the case, for example, in Pennsylvania, where the ACIR's study of Allegheny County/Pittsburgh found little or no use of special legislation to adapt statewide enabling rules to fit local circumstances or to resolve local metropolitan problems.[23] Ironically, state constitutional provisions intended to support local home rule can stand in the way of the local adaptation of statewide rules.

A METROPOLITAN CIVIL SOCIETY

Although the term ordinarily used to characterize a highly differentiated local public economy is "fragmentation," such a system need not "fragment" a metropolitan community. "Fragmentation" is a term that mixes description with evaluation. It is one thing to say that a metropolitan area contains a large number of provision units; it is another to say that the multiplicity of provision units "fragments" the metropolitan community. The degree of fragmentation is usually measured, both by proponents and opponents of metropolitan government, as a ratio of the number of jurisdictions to population. By itself, however, the measurement says nothing about the *fragmenting effect* of multiple jurisdictions. If the metropolis is viewed as a community of communities, there is nothing inherently fragmenting about a differentiated local public economy. Rather, differentiation may express the nature of metropolitan community more fully than would consolidation. The important question is whether *governmental fragmentation*, as conventionally measured, necessarily stands in the way of *metropolitan integration* through other means.

Broadly speaking, civil society embraces all those social relationships constituted on the basis of willing consent, rather than coercion. If the establishment of metropolitan government is viewed as the triumph of the "local state,"[24] as some scholars would term it, the governance structures of highly differentiated metropolitan areas represent the triumph of local civil society. Daniel J. Elazar refers to a metropolitan "civil community," constituted on the basis of intergovernmental and interorganizational relationships.[25] In 1972 Elazar noted that while "the civil community has no formal status in law, it has carved a place for itself in the constitutional system that is just now coming to be recognized and has yet to be precisely defined."[26] Although local governments clearly partake of coercion, overlying the numerous local governments of a metropolitan area—superimposed on them—is a *metropolitan civil society*, constituted by a network of voluntary agreements and associations among local officials and citizens. This web of social and political relationships is arguably the primary mechanism of metropolitan governance in America.

When Parks and Oakerson studied St. Louis and Allegheny Counties for the ACIR, they encountered metropolitan civil societies of great energy and vitality.[27] Both metro areas find common means of expression in areawide or countywide associations of municipalities, of fire chiefs and police chiefs, and of school districts and civic organizations. From these forums flow legitimate metropolitan perspectives on common issues, frequently leading to problem identification and areawide or countywide solutions. In St. Louis County, for example, most of the cooperative arrangements among local governments that sustain integrated production of key service components as well as pervasive patterns of mutual aid (discussed in chapter 4) emerged from voluntary associations of municipalities or local officials. Similar arrangements have emerged from regional Councils of Governments (COGs) in Allegheny County. Furthermore, the inclusion of the City of Pittsburgh in Allegheny County encourages the formation of public-private consortia that integrate central city and suburban interests in the common cause of economic development.

Occasionally, agreements reached within the metropolitan civil society require the imprimatur of law to be sustained—either to overcome the opposition of a few holdouts or to deter future free-riders. In this circumstance, St. Louis County has recourse to state law, accessed through the county delegation to the state legislature. Special state legislation for St. Louis County is common, with the support of the county's delegation. Given traditional legislative deference on local bills, the delegation becomes the formal keeper of the rules that sustain and advance a metropolitan civil society.

It is civil society that sustains metropolitan governance without recourse to a metropolitan government. The ideal arrangement of metro-reformers would create a single provision unit for an entire metropolitan community. A local public economy, on the other hand, generally consists of a variety of provision units—small and large. A monopoly provision unit would, almost certainly, be suboptimal. Instead of conceiving of metropolitan governance in terms of large general-purpose governments capable of both provision and production, one can think in terms of citizens and officials who maintain a metropolitan civil society common to multiple jurisdictions. When civil society is able to gain access to overlying governmental units—county and state—the result is a metropolitan governance structure capable of effectively addressing many areawide problems. As Elazar points out, a metropolitan civil society is potentially much more autonomous than any single unit of local government can or should be.[28]

Civil society does, however, follow certain governmental boundaries. County boundaries, in particular, seem to be important for defining the effective scope of metropolitan civil society. The most important institutional difference between metropolitan St. Louis and metropolitan Pittsburgh, for example, is found in the jurisdictional relationship between central city and county governments. St. Louis City and County are separate, nonoverlapping jurisdictions (St. Louis City is in effect its own county), while Pittsburgh is nested within Allegheny County. As a result, metropolitan civil society in Allegheny County more effectively integrates central city and suburban concerns and interests than it does in the St. Louis area. City-county competition and conflict in the St. Louis area parallel strong city-county cooperation in Allegheny County. The differing scope of civil society in the two metro areas is reflected in the sharply different economic conditions of their central cities.[29]

METROPOLITAN DYNAMICS AND ADAPTATION: THE ROLE OF PUBLIC ENTREPRENEURSHIP

One of the basic citizen choices in a metropolitan area is the choice of residence. Once provision units are in place, residents can take the characteristics of different communities into account in making relocation decisions. The ability of residents to sort themselves among diverse communities on the basis of individual preferences is an important dynamic in a local public economy. Charles M. Tiebout demonstrated that residential mobility has the potential, subject to various constraints, to achieve an optimal allocation of resources in the provision of local public goods and services.[30] Historical choices of boundaries therefore tend to be self-perpetuating. Once a set of jurisdictional boundaries has been determined, individuals make locational decisions accordingly, and tend over time to increase the efficiency of existing boundaries (i.e., the ability of a set of boundaries to satisfy a diverse set of individual preferences). The greater the number of choices available, the greater the effect of residential sorting. Yet existing boundaries can also become obsolete, as preferences become either more homogeneous or more heterogeneous or as organizational/operating costs either increase or decrease, and the resulting trade-offs change.

The maintenance of an efficient local public economy over time depends on structural flexibility and the continued availability of alternative arrangements in both provision and production. A local public economy is not static. In addition to obsolescence discussed above, the sources of change include shifting citizen preferences for goods and services, population growth (or loss), and developing technology. The latter includes not only "hardware" but also the softer kind of technology associated with "know-how." Economic change in local public economies is a vector of these forces. Efficiency in both provision and production depends on continued institutional adaptation to the complex change vector.

On the production side, the availability of alternatives increases producer competition. In a local *public* economy, however, the competition is not simply among private vendors, but between public and private vendors, as well as among public vendors of services. If competition among private suppliers is constrained (which can be the case if there are substantial economies of scale in production), it may be important to maintain the option of public production even if private production seems to be a better alternative at a given point in time. Maintaining the public option may mean, in turn, choosing *not* to contract out everything that could be contracted out. Maintaining a competitive environment could also mean, for a large provision unit, choosing to divide up the production of some service among different contractors rather than contracting with a single vendor. Where there are a number of small provision units, on the other hand, competition on the production side tends to be self-generating.

Adaptation not only requires alternatives, it also requires development of new alternatives. In short, it depends on innovation. The development of new arrangements for both provision and production is a key to adaptation and productivity improvement—also, in turn, a source of change. In a local public economy innovation depends on *public entrepreneurship*.[31] Like its private counterpart, a necessary condition of public entrepreneurship is initiative. Entrepreneurial potential can be measured by the number of possible sources of initiative in a local public economy. Counting the number of police chiefs, fire chiefs, directors of public works, city administrators or managers, and school superintendents yields a crude measure of the potential for public entrepreneurship in each service sector.

Also like the work of private entrepreneurs, public entrepreneurship must operate within external constraints in order to be productive. Private entrepreneurship operates best within the constraint of a competitive market, where consumers and their choices govern. Public entrepreneurship operates best within the constraint of a differentiated local public economy—the fragmented metropolis—where citizen choices also govern. However, citizen choice refers not merely to "exit" opportunities, changing one's place of residence, but to the use of citizen voice—amplified through close personal contact with elected representatives and frequent opportunities to participate in local referenda on basic issues of provision and governance.[32]

Public entrepreneurs potentially face high transaction costs as they seek agreements across multiple jurisdictions, obstacles that could discourage even the most persistent among them. Usually, there is little or no profit motive to offer an entrepreneurial incentive. Transaction costs are limited, however, by the metropolitan civil society. Civil associations of local governments, officials, and citizens facilitate public entrepreneurship by providing a convenient forum for its exercise. While governmental fragmentation creates numerous sources of initiative, metropolitan civil society provides the integrative forums that limit transaction costs. The result is a high level of public entrepreneurship. St. Louis County offers numerous illustrations, where police chiefs, fire chiefs, and school superintendents have created many successful joint production efforts, including an educational consortium for the application of computer technology in schools and a number of drug-enforcement units maintained jointly by several groups of municipal police departments.[33]

Adaptability and innovation must extend also to the provision side. Provision alternatives are sustained in several ways. One way consists of creating "nested" provision units with somewhat overlapping authority to act. The nesting of municipalities within a county is a common example. As general-purpose governments, municipalities and counties generally have overlapping or redundant authority to act even while sorting out their responsibilities on an informal basis. Provision units, like all human creations, are imperfect. If one unit fails to respond to constituents, a jurisdiction with redundant authority is then available. A form of political competition exists between officials, such as mayors and county commissioners, whose jurisdictions overlap, allowing "voter sovereignty" (analogous to consumer sovereignty) to exercise a choice between them. Incorporation, dissolution, annexation, and consolidation procedures all provide adaptability.[34] Overlapping jurisdictions enable citizens to re-sort responsibilities among both existing and potential units—to transfer functions. Functional transfer is an important and flexible tool of local governance, but its use depends upon the potential variety of provision units. Municipal incorporation or special-district formation not only creates a new unit but also transfers a limited set of functions from existing units to the newly created governmental unit. If the menu of possibilities has insufficient variety, it is also possible to ask the state legislature to create a new type of provision unit to be established at local option. BIDs are the most recent product of this sort of innovation.

Citizen frustrations over the past decade or so in Los Angeles, Milwaukee, Boston, and New York City underscore the difficulties that affect efforts to differentiate provision within large central cities. Residents of a high-crime area just south of downtown Los Angeles considered creating a special taxing district in 1987 to enhance police protection. Voters defeated the proposal after city hall agreed to increase the number of police officers deployed in the area.[35] Citizens in Milwaukee have actively considered the creation of a separate school district, centered upon a single high school that would serve a portion of the city's predominantly black population. Such a change would require new state legislation.[36] In 1986 voters in Boston defeated a proposal by residents of a predominantly black, 12.5 square-mile area to secede in order to form a separate municipality of "Mandela."[37] To allow citizens of Mandela to incorporate without securing approval from voters in the rest of Boston would also require new state legislation. In New York City, residents of Staten Island have also sought to secede. One possible problem with secession in this case is the absence of an overlying general-purpose government that would continue to tie Staten Island to the citizens of New York City for some limited set of purposes. Solving basic problems of service provision in the nation's major urban centers requires renewed attention to the capabilities of citizens to make boundary changes and, especially, to choose their primary local government units, while at the same time, establishing appropriate umbrella jurisdictions to take account of common problems and interests.

MAINTAINING METROPOLITAN EQUITY

One difficulty posed by a large number and variety of provision units in a local public economy is the emergence of inequalities in provision. Some communities inevitably have a greater ability than others to raise their own revenue to support public services. In fact, provision-side efficiency necessarily implies differences in spending. If communities have different preferences, those differences will be reflected in levels of spending from local revenues. At the same time, however, principles of equity in a democratic society suggest that there ought to be limits to the permissible range of inequality, although no objective definition of those limits is possible.

Some metropolitan reformers appear to accept much of the argument against consolidation based on efficiency, but continue to promote metropolitan government on equity grounds. From this perspective the problem reduces to a rather severe trade-off—efficiency versus equity. Choosing fragmentation brings efficiency with inequity; choosing consolidation brings equity with inefficiency. These are unpleasant terms of choice, to be avoided if possible. The important question is whether local public economies can be designed to avoid such a severe trade-off, or at least to reduce its severity.

The traditional approach to reducing fiscal disparity has emphasized the development of balanced communities, namely, metropolitan jurisdictions whose residents are heterogeneous with respect to income or wealth. This leads, at the metropolitan level, to metropolitan government. Yet such an approach is inconsistent with efforts to attain provision-side efficiency in terms of criteria such as fiscal equivalence and preference rev-elation. An alternative method of redistribution is to permit inequalities to develop among multiple provision units, such as municipalities and school districts, but to correct inequalities perceived as inequities through grants from overlapping jurisdictions, principally, state and federal govern-ments but perhaps county governments as well. The possibility exists that intergovernmental grants are more effective instruments of redistribution than governmental consolidation—this, because intergovernmental trans-fers allow recipient communities to be organized as independent provision units, able to make their own spending decision and work out their own production arrangements.

Alternative Approaches to Fiscal-Disparity Problems[38]

One difficulty with discussions of "inequity" is the often-implied standard of equality, which demands homogeneity. Yet provision-side efficiency nec-essarily implies a degree of inequality or heterogeneity of provision as long as the economic demand for public goods and services is variable. Equality and equity are not, however, the same.[39] One widely used principle of dis-tributive equity assumes inequality. This principle, developed by John Rawls,[40] evaluates a process or change by its treatment of the "least advan-taged" groups in a society. The question then is, "How do alternative governance arrangements in a metropolitan area affect the least advantaged members of a society?" Various benchmarks can be used for comparison, including the treatment of median-advantaged and most advantaged groups. Such an approach in principle allows us to examine the distribu-tional effects of alternative provision arrangements without having to use absolute equality as a standard. Inequalities in spending become inequitable when they reflect a systematic bias against the least advantaged—the poor.

It is axiomatic that the greater the number of non-overlapping provi-sion units in a local public economy, the greater will be the variation in average household income across those units. Consolidating provision units, and thus averaging over greater numbers of households, reduces the variation across units. The variation among households aggregated over all units remains exactly the same. These statistical differences do not imply that a greater number of local jurisdictions cause greater economic "segre-gation" among residential communities. Residents tend to sort themselves among neighborhoods according to income whether or not neighborhoods are organized as separate jurisdictions.

Nevertheless, the existence of fiscal inequalities among multiple provi-sion units does imply a need for intergovernmental transfers to relieve the inequities that may develop. Historically, the ACIR favored an approach that emphasized the development of well-balanced, heterogeneous communities, as local government jurisdictions able to pool resources from different income classes and provide services equitably, according to need.[41] This approach sought to avoid reliance on redistributive transfers primarily on the ground that it is politically more difficult to achieve interjurisdictional equity than it is to achieve intrajurisdictional equity in a fiscally balanced community. Yet it has proven to be much more difficult, politically, to consolidate local jurisdictions than to undertake fiscal transfers from overlapping jurisdictions. Local communities have found that it is not necessary to give up their jurisdictional autonomy, neither in order to benefit from redistribution nor to support less fortunate communities.

It is also difficult to wrap a local boundary around the equity problem. Creating a metropolitan jurisdiction may address inequalities within a metropolitan area, but it does nothing for differences between metropolitan and nonmetropolitan areas, or between different metropolitan areas. How far must local boundaries be expanded? Local jurisdictions, even if highly consolidated, are likely to fall somewhat short of being fully able to encapsulate the problem of fiscal equity.

The basic economic difficulty with an intrajurisdictional approach to redistribution, however, is its incompatibility with efforts to attain provision-side efficiency. The criterion of fiscal equivalence (discussed in chapter 1) is based on distributing services to communities in proportion to the revenues raised from those communities. Fiscal equivalence is also a standard of equity—market equity. The redistributive purpose of developing a balanced, heterogeneous community is just the opposite: to use revenues raised from one community to provide services to another. This can lead to a conclusion that the objectives of efficiency and market equity are fundamentally in conflict with redistributive equity, requiring a severe trade-off between competing values. There is, however, an alternative approach, available in highly differentiated local public economies.

This approach first allows provision units (municipalities or school districts, perhaps) to form on the basis of citizen preferences, thus allowing citizens to make efficient provision arrangements—those that can best satisfy their preferences—based on market equity. This permits inequalities to develop. Then more inclusive, overlapping jurisdictions (states or counties, perhaps) can correct for unacceptable inequalities through intergovernmental grants. Two advantages follow from this approach. First, provision-side efficiency can be obtained, within the limits of equity. Standards of equity are used to establish limits, within which local citizens are free to maximize their preference satisfaction, but are not used to override citizen choices by consolidating local jurisdictions. Second, the values and resources of an entire state or nation—communities much more inclusive and heterogeneous than any local jurisdiction—can then be used to guide and support redistribution, relieving local jurisdictions, at least in part, of the redistributive burden.

When comparing fiscal disparities in a highly differentiated (or fragmented) local public economy with those of a more consolidated set of jurisdictions, the appropriate base of comparison is not the fiscal disparity that exists as a matter of own-source revenues, but the disparity that remains after intergovernmental transfers. Fragmentation *without* overlap would be unable to resolve problems of fiscal disparity; fragmentation *with* overlap—the core of federalism—is a jurisdictional arrangement with greater ability to address efficiency and equity concerns simultaneously.

This conclusion is underscored by a recognition that equity problems are not confined to *fiscal* disparities across jurisdictions; equity problems also occur as *service* disparities within jurisdictions. The expenditure side of local government is at least as relevant to equity as the tax side. What is more, the efficiency with which money is spent and the responsiveness of service provision to community preferences intervene between taxes and expenditures, on the one side, and equity outcomes, on the other. *Equity is an attribute of service outcomes as well as tax and expenditure outcomes.* Fiscal disparity among local governments is at most an intermediate indicator of equity. Its relationship to service outcomes, and thus finally to equity, depends upon a host of other factors.

The attainment of equity in local service provision is, unfortunately, a complex problem. If it were possible to achieve equity simply by reducing disparities in revenue potential, then any pattern of organization that tended to increase those disparities would earn a negative rating on equity in its overall scorecard. Matters are not, however, so simple.

Empirical Research

Several unanswered empirical questions are at issue in the equity debate. How do differences *among* jurisdictions in a highly differentiated local public economy compare to differences among communities or neighborhoods *within* local jurisdictions, especially in large cities? How do fiscal disparities among jurisdictions compare to service disparities within jurisdictions? Moreover, how do intergovernmental fiscal transfers affect this comparison? Which pattern of organization—fragmentation or consolidation—provides for better "trusteeship" of intergovernmental revenues? Existing studies, while not conclusive, begin to shed light on these questions.

If one examines the own-source revenue potential of local jurisdictions in the more highly differentiated local public economies found in the suburban regions of metropolitan areas, considerable variation in "fiscal capacity" is apparent. Mark Schneider and John R. Logan,[42] who analyzed 1970–72 data for 1,139 municipalities in thirty-one Standard Metropolitan Statistical Areas (SMSAs), reported the very rich to be the most highly segregated group (dominant in 201 municipalities), followed by the very poor (dominant in 192 municipalities). The dispersion of the very poor was also somewhat greater than the very rich throughout other municipalities. A total of 746 municipalities in this study, however, were dominated by neither the very rich nor the very poor. Of this number, only sixty-six municipalities are dominated by any particular income class, leaving *the vast majority of suburban municipalities with a diverse population by income*. A picture of suburbia as highly segregated by income class turned out to be inaccurate, except for enclaves of the very rich and the very poor.[43]

Own-source revenue potential, however, represents only an *initial* distribution of resources. When intergovernmental transfers are taken into account, the picture that emerges is still different. Schneider and Logan report that, in 1972, the *total* revenue and expenditures of the very poor jurisdictions in their sample *exceeded* that of middle income municipalities and even, slightly, that of the very rich.[44] Substantially, however, this finding is due to greater expenditures on social services, including housing and hospitals, in poorer communities.[45] In 1972, federal aid as a percentage of cities' own-source revenues was only 10.8 percent. This figure increased to a high of 25.8 percent in 1978, but had fallen to 13.1 percent by 1985.[46] One of the disadvantages of relying on federal grants-in-aid to help distressed communities is perhaps the relative instability of assistance.

The ACIR study of St. Louis County used two different approaches in an effort to ascertain the presence of possible inequities among citizens residing in ninety municipalities.[47] First, the analysis included a search for "patterned inequalities," namely, variations in total revenue per municipality correlated with indicators of individual advantage or disadvantage in society. Three indicators were used: (1) median household income, (2) percent of population below poverty, and (3) percent of population nonwhite. None of the coefficients were significant. Revenue disparities among St. Louis County municipalities (after intergovernmental transfers) were not strongly patterned along income or racial lines. Second, however, the analysis also identified a small set of municipalities characterized by high tax burden (residential source revenues per household as a percentage of median household income) and low, total per-capita revenue, suggesting possible inequities. Overall, tax burden was related both to race and to age—citizens who were nonwhite and in their senior years tended to bear greater tax burdens, after adjusting for income differences and other community characteristics, than did other citizens. This analysis suggests that some scope still exists for redistribution to correct inequitable tax burdens in St. Louis County, even though disparities in revenues were not strongly patterned along lines of race or income.[48]

Studies of resource distribution within large centralized urban jurisdictions have generated mixed results. Various studies have found that large central-city jurisdictions tend to spend (a) more on police,[49] (b) less on streets,[50] and (c) less on libraries[51] in poor neighborhoods than in other neighborhoods. One well-known study of Oakland, California, found that the distribution of resources within the public school system followed a U-shaped curve. More resources were allocated to schools for the very poor and the very rich than for "middle-class" schools.[52] Even so, the existence of a single, large jurisdiction that moves *resources* from the very rich to the very poor does not necessarily mean that poor communities will actually be better off in *benefit* terms. Numerous studies have found that the quality of urban public education, for instance, is considerably lower in poor neighborhoods than in others.[53]

The Problem of Redistribution

Research on the relationship between jurisdiction size and the efficiency and responsiveness of provision units (discussed in chapter 3) at least suggests the possibility that smaller jurisdictions may be better trustees of fiscal resources. If this is the case, *inter*jurisdictional fiscal transfers may be preferred to *intra*jurisdictional transfers as a means of addressing equity concerns. It follows that expanding the boundaries of local government jurisdictions may not promote greater equity as effectively as reducing fiscal disparities through intergovernmental sharing.

This conclusion is fundamentally at odds with a widespread belief about metropolitan relationships, namely, that suburban autonomy is a major *cause* of central-city fiscal distress. The argument made is that wealthier residents fled to the suburbs precisely to avoid having to pay for services to poorer residents, allowing them to tax themselves exclusively for the purpose of providing their own high-quality services. Wealthy suburban residents then continued to derive benefits from their proximity to a major city without having to support it financially. To overcome this perceived equity problem, reformers frequently proposed that central cities be given unilateral annexation powers and that municipal incorporation in suburban areas be restricted.

Differing interpretations can be placed, however, on the so-called "flight to the suburbs." The wealthy are not alone in this movement; middle- and lower-income residents have joined the exodus from cities. Those who move may be reacting to more than urban redistribution; they may also be reacting to a loss of control over their immediate communities. Perhaps urban citizens object not so much to redistribution as to their inability to target any portion of their tax revenue to their own communities. A major attraction of the suburbs is surely the greater ability to allocate resources to one's own community—regardless of the redistribution that may also occur. In fact, suburban residents do not escape redistributive taxation; redistribution cannot be avoided as long as more inclusive jurisdictions—county, state, and federal—support it. What they do gain is much greater control over local taxes and expenditures. This is the suburban advantage, one not confined to a few small enclaves of the very wealthy. The fiscal imbalance between suburbs and central cities may therefore be a function of urban governance arrangements, in particular the political monopoly enjoyed by city hall. Expanding central-city boundaries would simply increase the monopoly power of city government, which is the underlying cause of the problem.

Political Choice for Disadvantaged Communities

The central problem with boundary expansion as a means of reducing inequities—whether it be an expanding central city or the consolidation of suburban municipalities—is the tendency to deprive communities— whether economically advantaged or disadvantaged—of an ability to make their own collective choices. In particular, consolidation tends to make economically disadvantaged communities into politically disadvantaged communities as well. The function of the provision side of a local public economy is not simply to raise revenue; it is also to enable residents to choose how to spend public revenue and, most importantly, to choose *how to arrange for production.* Poor communities without this choice may see their scarce resources consumed by urban bureaucracies that return little benefit. Relying upon intrajurisdictional transfers deprives recipient communities of the ability to make these "provision-side" choices. It may also disable poor communities from seeking more equitable treatment from county and state jurisdictions through their own elected officials. Simply because poor communities may not be able to raise all of their own revenue is no reason to deprive them still further of the ability to function as a provision unit. Receiving public funds by interjurisdictional transfer is a function that requires a provision unit. The choice of a provision unit for this purpose obviously does not have to be driven by the ability to raise revenue.

In many central cities it may be necessary to create new provision units—or rather, to allow for their creation by citizens—if only for the purpose of *receiving public funds*. This alone would break the monopoly power of city hall, at least with respect to disadvantaged communities. ACIR recommendations on the formation of neighborhood governments address the potential for this pattern of organization.[54] The logic of BIDs, discussed in chapter 3, can also be extended to include problems of urban development in poor neighborhoods. Suburban residents may be more inclined to support metropolitan redistribution if (1) it does not threaten their local autonomy and (2) it is targeted to poor communities that need it the most. There are in fact self-interested reasons for wealthy and middle-income communities in a metropolitan area to help their less fortunate neighbors: suburbanites are not in the long run well served by a deteriorating central city. Self-interested metropolitan residents are likely to look upon effective urban development programs not as redistribution but as a smart investment in the common future of the entire metro area. But self-interest requires that the money be well spent and well targeted. Sending more money downtown to be spent by city hall may not inspire confidence in suburban residents.

The mitigation of local fiscal disparities need not be a responsibility reserved exclusively to state and national governments. Metropolitan-area resource sharing is also possible—the prime example being a partial sharing of the commercial and industrial property tax base pioneered by the Minneapolis-St. Paul metropolitan community.[55] By partially sharing the revenue growth from economic development, the emergence of fiscal disparities among local jurisdictions is constrained. Other metropolitan communities should be studied to ascertain the extent to which fiscal disparities can be mitigated by the policies of local overlapping jurisdictions and by adjustments in the fiscal rules of local governance, including local revenue diversification.[56]

Historically, the ACIR closely monitored metropolitan fiscal disparities.[57] The research challenge today is to compare interjurisdictional disparities—between governments—to neighborhood disparities within jurisdictions, especially central cities. Only then can we know the real terms of the trade-off between fragmentation and consolidation. The performance of both fragmented and consolidated areas, however, includes the performance of the fiscal-transfer system. Future research should also study both the instruments of fiscal transfer used by overlapping jurisdictions, including state and federal grant-in-aid formulas, and the performance of provision units (including big and small cities) that receive funds. At issue is the ability of both granting and receiving jurisdictions to focus assistance on those communities in greatest need.

THE PROBLEM OF REDEVELOPMENT

One of the better known hypotheses relating metropolitan governance to central-city viability is based on the concept of the "elastic city," popularized in recent years by David Rusk, former mayor of Albuquerque, New Mexico.[58] Rusk argues that when central cities enjoy unilateral powers of annexation, they can easily expand as the urban area grows, thus maintaining a stronger tax base and discouraging racial segregation in separate local jurisdictions. He arrays evidence based on a series of comparisons between elastic and inelastic cities, in an effort to show that the elastic city in each pair performs better on a set of criteria including, especially, economic growth.

Rusk's methodology, however, has some difficulties. Differences in central-city prosperity are also strongly affected by exogenous factors, such as the age and location of the city. To compare old established cities of the urban Northeast with the newer cities of the sun-laden Southwest is to compare the proverbial apples and oranges. Yet this is exactly what two of Rusk's seven pairs do, comparing Detroit to Houston and Syracuse to Albuquerque and attributing the observed differences to "elasticity." In each pair elastic cities are located in metro-areas that experience much higher rates of population growth than their inelastic counterparts (13). The relationship he discovers between elasticity and growth is most likely spurious, accounted for by age and location among other uncontrolled factors. When Rusk goes on to report that "elastic areas have higher rates of job creation" and "elastic areas show greater gains in real income" (42–43), he has drawn conclusions based on what may be mainly statistical artifacts derived from the higher rates of metro-area growth for the elastic cities in each pair. While his pair-wise comparisons serve a rhetorical and illustrative purpose if the aim is to persuade, they may also be misleading if the aim is to discover empirical relationships. Rusk endeavored to match the cities in each pair on the basis of the absolute number of new home-buyers, as well as the percent of metro-population that is black (11). He argues that the number of new home-buyers is the key to the growth of local jurisdictions. Obviously, if a central city has fixed boundaries and is already densely populated, new growth will occur outside its boundaries. A densely populated city may even lose population as residents search for less concentrated living conditions. Rusk's first law of urban dynamics, that "only elastic cities grow" (10) merely states a truism: a city that is full of people cannot hold more people.

By Rusk's standards, both Pittsburgh and the City of St. Louis are inelastic. Yet their economic performance is dramatically different. Fragmentation clearly has not deterred economic growth in St. Louis County, but city-county separation does hurt the City. Pittsburgh, by contrast, has been the centerpiece of county-led development efforts, helping to transform its economy. Clearly, some factor other than central-city elasticity is at work, arguably the jurisdictional relationship between city and county. Moreover, Allegheny County is fully incorporated. There are no elastic jurisdictions, even in the suburbs, though of course there are differences in population density, allowing for new development. Pittsburgh's success in redevelopment relied on a strong, *noncompetitive* county government, accomplishing exactly what Rusk argues an inelastic city cannot do. Central-city elasticity is *not* a necessary condition of central-city success.

More generally, Rusk's analysis neglects the fact that most suburban municipalities, especially in the long-established metropolitan areas of the Northeast, are as inelastic as central cities. Each suburb is surrounded by others, and, although not as densely developed as the central city, does not seek to grow, but only to maintain its population. By Rusk's own logic, inelastic suburban communities should be in even worse shape than the central city; in fact, of course, some are, e.g., numerous former steel-mill towns just south of Pittsburgh.

One of the major problems that Rusk is attending to, however, is real: it is the problem of urban *redevelopment*. Urban capital stock is without exception subject to obsolescence, though for a variety of reasons, including natural deterioration from age, changing tastes and preferences in living and shopping styles, and structural economic changes. Central city neighborhoods are hardly alone in the recurrent need for redevelopment. Much of the redevelopment task can be handled by private investment, but not all. Deteriorating streets, bridges, sidewalks, water mains, sewers, parks— public infrastructure—also need to be redeveloped. More importantly, private and public redevelopment efforts often have to be coordinated. The redevelopment of a residential area may depend on access to appropriate residential amenities, provided by local government. An obsolescent community cannot usually supply its own redevelopment capital. Its ability to borrow may be greatly limited by uncertainty regarding its future. Redevelopment is therefore at least a metropolitan-level problem, one that requires pooling revenue on a countywide or metro-wide basis for highly targeted use in the redevelopment of selected communities. No jurisdiction is completely immune from this problem over the long run; all communities in a metro-area therefore have a long-term interest in addressing the problem effectively.

One way to respond to the redevelopment problem is to grease the expansion of central cities—this means either unilateral annexation or, in the case of central cities already ringed by suburbs, forced consolidation. This is the solution called for by many voices, not only David Rusk's. However, the price that would have to be paid for such a solution is high.

It includes significant inefficiencies on both the provision and production sides of a local public economy, as well as a substantial loss of local self-government and attendant opportunities for civic engagement. While this trade-off is perhaps difficult to assess, it is also unnecessary.

The alternative is to rely on metropolitan civil society and its governance structures. As discussed above, however, civil society does follow overlying governmental boundaries, and the existence of a large overlying jurisdiction that includes the central city is essential if central-city problems are to be effectively addressed. It is important that the overlying jurisdiction be *noncompetitive* with the municipalities under its jurisdictional umbrella. St. Louis County, by contrast, has been competitive not only with St. Louis City but also with its own municipalities, seeking to build its own version of a municipality in the unincorporated area of the county. The absence of unincorporated territory in Allegheny County facilitates county cooperation with all its municipalities, including Pittsburgh. County government must stand to gain, unambiguously, from the growth of the various municipalities in its jurisdiction. In the case of Pittsburgh, its ties with county government have also been strengthened historically by common allegiance to the Democratic Party, which controlled both city hall and the county courthouse. In other cases it might be necessary to create a countywide or metro-wide redevelopment district—a special-purpose government—for the purpose of reinvesting in community infrastructure. Various state and federal aid funds could be channeled through such a district as well. The governance of such a district should be carefully designed so as to provide broad representation of communities and neighborhoods through the area. Within central cities, BIDs or similar jurisdictions can be relied on to make application for redevelopment funds and then provide for the maintenance of redeveloped infrastructure. Much of the work might best be carried out under the direction of task forces that bring together county and city governments, community representatives, civic organizations, and local business and labor groups.

CONCLUSION

Metropolitan governance does not require metropolitan government. It can and does emerge in highly fragmented metropolitan areas. Such a governance process relies on *areawide rules* to assign authority among local governments; a *metropolitan civil society* to integrate the metropolis across multiple jurisdictions through a web of voluntary agreements and associations; and *collective choice by citizens* to constitute the provision side of a local public economy. Highly interactive and minimally hierarchical, it is a mode of governance both consistent with a highly differentiated local public economy and capable of areawide problem solving, including the alleviation of inequalities and the redevelopment of worn-out infrastructure. It supports high levels of citizen engagement and public entrepreneurship, at the same time encouraging citizens and local officials to look not only to their own interests but to the interests of others as well. This would seem to be at the least a salutary process, not one deserving of the wholesale condemnation heaped on it by its reformist critics. Arguably, it is one deserving of preservation, improvement, elaboration, and extension.

6

THE CIVIC METROPOLIS

INTRODUCTION

Two major points of view have dominated the metropolitan debate. One sees the metropolis as a single community in need of a single metropolitan government; the other sees the metropolis as a marketplace in which mobile residents shop for local governments in much the same way they shop for groceries. Both perspectives reveal important truths. Common interests shared on a metropolitan scale do suggest the need for some form of metropolitan governance; at the same time, local communities do to some extent compete for residents and their tax dollars, creating pressures for greater efficiency—pressures that a single metropolitan government would eviscerate. Both perspectives also, however, miss a great deal. Both fail to see the elaborate production structures worked out in specific service sectors to capture economies of scale while avoiding diseconomies. Both fail to see the advantages associated with the organizational variety of local government and the ability of the metropolis to draw simultaneously on different governmental forms—from overlying county to local village to special districts of every stripe. Both fail to see the public entrepreneurship exercised both within and across service sectors by local police chiefs, fire chiefs, school superintendents, city managers, and many others. Both fail to see the extensive patterns of cooperation that tie separate jurisdictions together in multiorganizational networks of service delivery. Both fail to see the extensive opportunities for civic engagement presented by a large number of local jurisdictions, including service as local public officials from citizen-mayor to school-board member. Both fail to see the metropolitan civil society composed of areawide voluntary associations that provide much of the governance structure needed to address areawide problems. Both fail to see the mechanisms used by local actors to prescribe areawide rules through state legislation, engendering a form of metropolitan governance without metropolitan government. Both fail to see the key role played by citizens—not simply as voters in local elections, nor as mobile residents selecting their local government of choice, but as direct participants in constitutive decisions that create and modify local jurisdictions and thereby shape the local public economy.

The theory and methodology of local public economies opens the way to a new understanding of metropolitan governance and how it works. Each local government is a public household, a local republic organized by citizens to represent a set of common interests. Diverse local governments represent somewhat different, often overlapping, interests. Like private households, public households choose whether to produce in-house, produce jointly with other households, or contract-out with independent producers, who may be public or private. As local governments make these decisions, they generate a local public economy—a set of relationships between the providers and producers of public goods and services. All of this occurs within a configuration of rules—a local-government constitution—used to govern the formation of provision and production units and their relationships. Depending on the rules and how well the rules fit local circumstances, local public economies are more or less efficient, more or less equitable, and more or less responsive to a variety of public interests.

At bottom, local public economies are civic expressions, driven by the choices and activities of citizens. A recognition of the essentially civic character of metropolitan governance has been largely missing from the metro-reform debate. The structure of metropolitan governance is a product of civic engagement together with a public philosophy intent on sustaining meaningful local government. Largely unrecognized within metropolitan America is a civic tradition of substantial importance to the nation. Obscured by intellectual biases against suburban development and shamed by the standard litany of metropolitan reform, still it survives. Erstwhile reformers who rail against a metropolitan structure based on multiple local governments need to recognize that this is a house that citizens built. Rather than a mark of the privatization of public life, the American system of local government is one that depends on the civic commitment of its citizens. The large number of small local governments found in both metropolitan and nonmetropolitan areas simply could not exist without a substantial commitment of time and energy by their citizens.

Because of the disparities in our understanding of the metropolis, the connection between social-science research and political reform in metropolitan America is often hard to find. Reformers continue to push for sweeping local-government consolidations that directly contradict the most careful research findings. The metro-government movement seems ever alive and well—inhabiting the editorial pages of major urban newspapers and enjoying as much support as ever among a host of good-government and professional groups. Sometimes only a handful of academics seem to be aware that the standard metro-government recommendations of forty years ago can no longer be supported on efficiency grounds.

The missing link is civics—shared knowledge and understanding among citizens. Specialized academic knowledge, when it pertains to a process fueled by citizen activity, can only be useful when it speaks to citizens—adopts their perspectives, addresses their needs, and serves their interests. Needed is a new metropolitan civics—a mode of inquiry and style of discourse designed to serve the knowledge requirements of local citizens. Research findings do not suggest that the status quo simply be maintained—not that metro-areas ever stand still. The civic metropolis is a dynamic structure, ever shifting as citizens and officials engage new problems. The study of local public economies can contribute to a reshaping of the metropolitan reform agenda—reinforcing the civic character of local governance and extending its logic to address deepening problems, such as the deterioration of urban neighborhoods in central cities.

This chapter begins with an interpretation of the major research findings to emerge from the study of metropolitan areas, goes on to consider principles of metropolitan governance consistent with research findings, and concludes with an agenda for continued research and reform. If they are to achieve their intended effects, reformers need to know what they are doing.

HOW FRAGMENTATION WORKS

The most revealing finding to emerge from metropolitan-area research in recent decades is this: fragmentation is associated not with higher, but with lower local government spending per capita. Numerous empirical studies have found this relationship.[1] Moreover, the relationship holds up when indicators of public demand for services are controlled, supporting an inference that *fragmentation is positively related to efficiency*—that fragmented metropolitan areas tend to be get more service from less spending (Figure 6.1).[2] The question that remains is—*why?* Why does more fragmentation produce lower spending and greater efficiency? How does fragmentation work?

Explaining the positive relationship between fragmentation and efficiency is of more than academic interest. Certainly the finding alone should at least give pause to aggressive and indiscriminate consolidation efforts. It

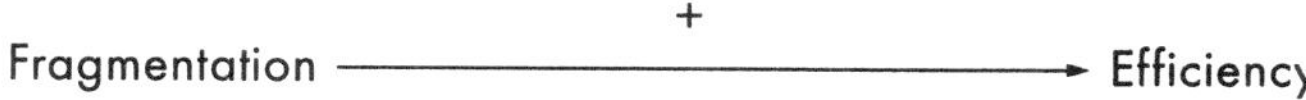

Figure 6.1
Positive relationship observed between fragmentation and efficiency in
metropolitan organization.

says clearly what *not* to do—don't push citizens to consolidate their local governments in order to save money—but it tells us little about what policy makers ought to do in order that metropolitan areas might work better. Recommendations to "increase fragmentation" are ambiguous—there are many different ways to do so—and fail to supply useful advice on precisely how to address problems in context. Local public economies develop by addressing quite specific problems in effective ways. Often this means increasing the measurable fragmentation of a metro-area, that is, increasing the number of local governments per capita, but sometimes it may mean just the opposite. Sound policy advice depends on understanding *how* fragmentation affects performance through a number of potential intervening variables.

More generally, research findings do not speak for themselves; they require interpretation. In particular, observing a relationship between two variables does not explain why the relationship occurs. One prominent method of interpretation in the social sciences consists of choice-based reasoning, which asks why individuals choose to act in the ways they do. Related to fragmentation, the question is this: what leads individuals in fragmented areas—both citizens and officials—to act in ways that constrain spending and increase efficiency?

The Standard Explanation: Local-Government Competition

The most common explanation of how fragmentation works is a variant of market competition widely associated with Charles M. Tiebout's pure theory of local expenditure. According to this theory, local governments compete for residents who "vote with their feet" to select the most desirable local governments, meaning those that offer a superior tax-service package. The process of residential choice induces greater local-government efficiency. This reasoning leads to a conception of fragmented metropolitan areas as *local-government markets*. Residents shop for local governments, and the resulting competition among governments leads to more efficient governmental behavior. The greater the fragmentation, the greater the potential competition among local governments and, thus, the more efficient the result. Most researchers who report an inverse relationship

Figure 6.2
Interlocal competition model explaining the positive relationship
between fragmentation and efficiency in metropolitan organization.

between fragmentation and per capita spending (or a positive relationship
between fragmentation and efficiency) rely on the Tiebout model to
explain the results. In this case, local-government competition becomes the
key intervening variable linking fragmentation to efficiency (see figure 6.2).

Critics of the interlocal competition model generally attack its assumptions—in particular, the assumption that individuals shop for governments
and make locational choices based on alternative tax-service packages—
and attempt to array evidence against it by trying to show that its
assumptions do not hold. Yet in one sense, this line of criticism is beside the
point. Attacking Tiebout's assumptions does nothing to discredit the empirical finding that fragmentation is associated with lower per capita spending
and greater efficiency. If the interlocal competition model is inadequate, it
is only because it cannot explain the finding. *The finding remains*—puzzling,
but no less empirically valid.

The difficulties with the interlocal competition model, however, are
not easily dismissed.[3] The explanation depends on assumptions of cost-less
entry and exit, plus either fully mobile assets or nonproperty taxation. Yet
the taxable property of homeowners—consisting mostly of real estate—is
largely immobile. Moreover, its immobility is one of the attractive features
of real estate as a local government tax base. Homeowners can exit from
a local jurisdiction, but they ordinarily cannot, turtle-like, carry their
dwelling with them. This severely limits the immediate impact of homeowner exit on local governments. Even if homeowners leave the community,
they continue to pay local property taxes until they can sell their property, at
which point the local government acquires another taxpayer to replace
the one it just lost. Imagine the effect on market competition if consumers
were required to supply replacement customers before they can take their
business elsewhere! Of course, the taxable value of local property may
decline; depending on the frequency of reassessment (critics of Tiebout,
take note), this effect does not depend on large numbers of movers. Yet a
decline in the local property tax base is a gradual, long-term process.
Market competition works because it generates immediate "cash-drawer"
effects, which punish uncompetitive, and reward competitive, behaviors.
Because the property tax blunts the cash-drawer effect of local-government

competition in the important case of homeowners, the efficacy of interlocal competition would seem to be greatly limited.

In other cases, however, Tiebout effects are more telling. Commercial and industrial property owners have taxable property that is considerably more mobile. A local firm that threatens to move out of a community has leverage supplied by the greater mobility of its capital. In another case, local jurisdictions that have a great deal of undeveloped land and seek to grow may compete for *added* residents on the basis of their tax-service packages. More generally, competition among local provision units increases the leverage of commercial and industrial firms and developers with local governments, but it is does not significantly enhance the leverage of current homeowners. If you doubt this, imagine the reaction at city hall if an especially critical homeowner, in his latest protest call to the mayor's office, threatens to move out of town! Tax-competition nevertheless does limit the extent to which local provision units can rely on commercial and industrial property for local revenue without supplying corresponding benefits. This is a significant constraint insofar as commercial and industrial property is a major source of financial support for local government. Moreover, increased interest in the encouragement of economic development has perhaps heightened this sort of competitive pressure.

Residential mobility is important, but not because it engenders competition for residents among local governments. Its contribution is to allow citizen-consumers to sort themselves among provision units on the basis of their tax-service preferences. Over time this self-sorting increases provision-side efficiency by grouping together residents with similar preferences. When it comes to obtaining political responsiveness to residents, however, "voting with your feet" is no substitute for local elections and political participation. Competition among local governments cannot be expected to limit the tax-prices of services to ordinary residents apart from the ability of citizens to impose a *political* constraint on officials. In the terms used by Albert O. Hirschman, "exit" cannot take the place of "voice."[4] This is why the governance of a local public economy depends on institutional arrangements that assign important *political roles* to citizens, as argued in chapter 5. Increasingly, citizen voice includes the approval of tax-rate increases by popular referendum, a device that would simply be redundant if local-government competition closely resembled market competition.

Alternative or Complementary Explanations

Rejecting the interlocal competition model as a full account of how fragmentation works, however, leaves a considerable puzzle. If not local-government competition, what does account for the observed negative correlation between fragmentation and spending? Several possible factors may be at work—all consistent with the ACIR field studies of St. Louis and Allegheny Counties.

One possibility is the greater degree of *fiscal equivalence* made possible by multiple provision units. When local communities can get what they pay for and must pay for what they get, the equivalence between taxes and services reduces fiscal illusion—the perception of getting something for nothing, that government services are free. The reduction of fiscal illusion constrains demand. When the *political* demand for services is limited by *economic* demand measured by willingness and ability to pay, responsive local governments spend less than they otherwise would. It should be noted, however, that fiscal equivalence requires only multiple taxing districts, not necessarily multiple local governments. A single local-government jurisdiction can achieve fiscal equivalence through the use of special taxing districts—provided the jurisdiction is responsive to more localized demands for services.

Another possibility is the *greater access to elected representatives* afforded citizens in more fragmented metropolitan areas. In St. Louis County, for example, some 873 local officials represent roughly a million citizens.[5] Greater access, it can be argued, leads to more effective citizen voice, and more effective voice leads to more favorable tax-service packages. When the incentives supplied to voters by means of fiscal equivalence are added to superior access to elected representatives, the result is a potentially powerful constraint on increases in local spending that lack corresponding benefits.

Moving to the production side, there are other possible explanatory factors. Multiple provision units, as argued in chapter 4, are more likely to build a *differentiated production structure* well matched to diverse economies of scale and supported by pervasive cooperation among local producers. Because only some service components benefit from large-scale production, more consolidated local governments often operate at a scale of production that is inefficiently large. Fragmented metropolitan areas, by contrast, generally exhibit production structures akin to the patterns of industrial organization found in the private sector. As a result, a more fragmented public sector would tend to operate more efficiently, reducing the costs of local government, just as research has shown.

Competition reemerges on the production side as a possible factor, but this time it is *competition among producers*, not among providers.[6] To the extent that local governments as provision units can draw on alternative producers of services or service components, competitive dynamics among producers will reduce service costs to local governments. For example, evidence of price competition was found among the producers of contract

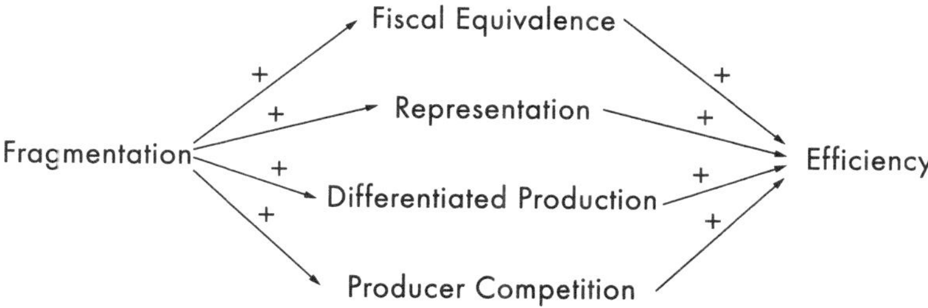

Figure 6.3
Public economy model explaining the positive relationship between
fragmentation and efficiency in metropolitan organization.

police services in St. Louis County.[7] Despite increases in contracting-out,
producer competition in local public economies remains quite limited, even
in the most highly fragmented areas. Patterns of competition among producers, however, do not seem sufficiently widespread to account for very
much aggregate expenditure reduction.

Each of these four possible factors links fragmentation to efficiency
without recourse to local-government competition as an explanation, as
displayed in figure 6.3. Fragmentation increases fiscal equivalence and
access to elected representatives, supports more differentiated production
structures, and allows producer competition—all of which increase efficiency. It follows that a *local public economy* is not identical to a *local
government market*. Differentiation in the local public economy—multiple
provision and production units linked in various ways—can contribute to
efficiency, without relying on competition among local governments as
providers. Even if local public economies are not best viewed as markets, an
economic theory of local government remains useful. Economic reasoning
and market-based reasoning are related but not identical. An economy
refers not just to markets but to a broad range of institutional arrangements
for relating demand to supply. Local public economies cannot be fully
understood as markets even though they draw significantly on market-based
and market-like relationships. Economic reasoning is best understood as
choice-based reasoning,[8] an effort to understand why individuals make the
choices they do in terms of the constraints and opportunities they face. The
alternative explanations offered above are all consistent with choice-based
reasoning; that is, they explain how metropolitan fragmentation affects the
choices that citizens and local officials make in efficiency-enhancing ways.

Little or no research has been done to test the alternative explanations,
in part because sorting out the effects of the various factors would not be

easy. Many of the relevant variables are highly intercorrelated. Such a research program, nevertheless, is quite important when considering metropolitan-area policy. If competition is all that matters, then the structure of metropolitan governance and the precise choice of provision and production structures are not policy issues of high salience. What matters instead is simply the number of competitors, and the most salient policy issues concern the rules of entry into a local government market. But if fiscal equivalence is important, local boundaries matter, and so do the institutions that structure the choice of boundaries. If access to elected representatives makes a difference, local-government structure matters, and so do the institutions that structure the formation of local governments. If efficient service production depends on an elaborate industrial structure of agencies, then relationships among local government agencies matter, and so do the institutions that structure those relationships. In general, a variety of institutional arrangements become policy concerns, affecting the performance of local public economies.

Instead of a market metaphor the public economy model suggests a civic interpretation of metropolitan organization. Fragmentation multiplies the ties between citizens and their local governments, creating numerous opportunities for residents to serve their communities, both as public officials and as private citizens. The multiplex relationships among people that sustain a sense of community then become a resource for local government as well. Not mobile consumers but committed citizens make fragmentation work. Highly mobile residents are less likely to care about the long-term prospects of community life. They are therefore less likely to invest the time and effort needed to contribute to community well-being. Without committed citizens willing to serve their communities, the fragmented metropolis would collapse for lack of willing hands to carry out the hard work of provision and governance. Arguably, suburban and rural America—where fragmentation is greatest—are heirs to the same civic-republican spirit that animated the American Revolution and that Alexis de Tocqueville observed at work in the 1830s.

NO ONE CORRECT PATTERN OF ORGANIZATION

A great deal of intellectual energy, spanning several decades, has been expended in efforts to determine the single correct pattern of organization for metropolitan areas. Numerous motivations contribute to these efforts—capturing economies of scale in production, achieving better service coordination, controlling spillover effects, and overcoming fiscal disparities. Whatever the motivation, however, the common goal of metropolitan reform has been to replace a complex "crazy-quilt" pattern of local jurisdictions with a simpler pattern that can be uniformly applied throughout a metropolitan area. Uniformity of service provision and production arrangements is the goal, whether sought through a single-tier, two-tier, or multi-tier design. This is thought to be the only way to achieve a coherent system of organization. Finding the "one right way" to organize metropolitan areas has often been, therefore, the central preoccupation of reform-minded scholars.

Historically, local citizens have usually resisted metropolitan reforms that entail substantial jurisdictional consolidation. It is important to try to understand why. Objective criteria, related to the scale of effect associated with the provision (or nonprovision) of a public good or service, can be used to establish a minimum-size provision unit. For many local public goods and services, however, this lower limit is quite small, consisting of what is ordinarily called a neighborhood. The outer limit on local boundaries derives from citizen preferences and the way in which preferences cluster geographically. There is no fully objective way of determining an appropriate set of provision units apart from the expressed preferences of local citizens for public goods and services. The ease with which a single provision unit can satisfy individual preferences decreases with the preference heterogeneity of the community. By the same token, the ability to satisfy diverse preferences increases with an increase in the number of provision units in a local public economy—at least up to some point. The creation of provision units is constrained by the expected transaction costs of organizing and operating an additional unit. Transaction costs include the costs of citizen participation. The choice is between greater preference satisfaction, obtained by creating an additional provision unit, and lower transaction costs. Citizens face a trade-off that only they can decide.

The same choice is faced in the dissolution of a provision unit. To take a nonmetropolitan example, recently a small rural village located in western New York chose to dissolve. The default unit of local government was the overlying town, which contained no other village. The dissolution was carefully negotiated between the two units even though the village could have dissolved unilaterally. Dissolution was supported by village officials and overwhelmingly approved by citizens. Upon dissolution, the town created a set of special tax districts with boundaries coterminous with the previous village boundaries, preserving fiscal equivalence. Most village employees became town employees. Few additional economies of scale in production could be captured because of pre-existing cooperation between village and town. The major change brought by dissolution was a reduction of transaction costs—one less unit of government to operate. Transaction costs consist mostly of time and effort, and it is mostly time and effort, not money, being saved in the former village. The price of dissolution is the potential for somewhat less responsive service provision. Village citizens decided, in effect, that the extra potential responsiveness was insufficient to compensate for the time and trouble required to make a separate unit of local government work.

The trade-off involved in the creation or dissolution of a provision unit is highly subjective. It is a trade-off that necessarily takes place in the minds of citizens. No amount of objective planning can substitute for a subjective trade-off, even though objective inquiries can supply important information useful to citizens in their decision making. Because only citizens can make a unit of local government work, it is their informed preferences that matter.

It is noteworthy, however, that the productivity of local governments depends on the willingness of citizens to absorb relatively high transaction costs. Such a willingness is an important ingredient of civic virtue. All communities face the difficulty that many of the benefits of citizen participation accrue less to the individual participant than to the community at large. When voluntary participation costly to individuals creates a public good beneficial to an entire community, citizens face free-rider temptations to "let George do it." Although communities can overcome some critical free-rider problems by creating local governments with access to coercive powers of taxation and regulation, they cannot use this expedient to sustain the level of citizen commitment and participation required to make a local government work. Communities unable to overcome these problems become candidates for consolidation. The maintenance of the social relationships that sustain communities and community-oriented local government requires constant attention and a lot of hard work on the part of local citizens.

From a governance standpoint, the key question in the organization of a local public economy is *who decides*, incrementally, whether to add or subtract a provision unit. The prevailing answer in the American system of local government is that *citizens decide*, one provision unit at a time. This is not simply "decentralization," whereby a central government creates a set of local government units for local citizens. This is the assignment of constitutional authority to local citizens, allowing the basic pattern of local-government organization to emerge from a series of local community choices. Local citizen choice is the constitutive principle of American local government.

From this line of reasoning, a "crazy-quilt" pattern of jurisdictions can be viewed as a coherent pattern of organization because it derives from a rational process of community formation. When allowed to choose, citizens in different communities make different choices. As a result, the pattern of organization that emerges from citizen choice is not uniform throughout a metropolitan area. Different communities arrive at different trade-offs. This means that some parts of a metropolitan area may provide services in one way, while others' parts choose different arrangements. By contrast, metropolitan reformers seek the same arrangements everywhere. The coexistence of fire protection districts with municipal fire departments in the same metropolitan area, for example, sends reformers to the drawing board. Yet the establishment of a uniform metropolitan-wide pattern implies that the same trade-off is appropriate for every citizen in every community. Little wonder that uniform decentralization schemes undertaken in various parts of the world often result in local governments that locals do not want and in which they refuse to participate.

A similar logic applies to the organization of the production side, except that more objective considerations are involved and local officials are the principal decision-makers. Production units can efficiently be added as long as the net cost of operating an additional unit is less than the benefit from greater specialization. The costs of additional units are in great part transaction costs. The key question is, again, who decides. If local officials decide (instead of central planners), the transaction costs are likely to be taken into account, so that new production arrangements represent real efficiency gains.

Instead of looking for one correct pattern of organization, metropolitan research should be concerned with variable patterns of governance and how governance relates—through the structure of a local public economy—to performance. The principal governance variables are "who decides" and under what conditions. Who decides—when new units are formed or old ones abandoned, consolidated, or "grown" through annexation? From these decisions emerges the structure of a local public economy—some number and variety of provision and production units. This structure, in turn, affects performance, judged according to multiple criteria, including both efficiency and equity. The process can be depicted as follows:

$$\text{Governance} \longrightarrow \text{Structure} \longrightarrow \text{Performance}$$

Judging structure directly on the single criterion of uniformity contributes little to the advancement of research or reform. The questions are how governance affects structure and how structure affects performance. As we learn, we accumulate the capability to diagnose problems and recommend incremental reforms. We can even learn how to "fix" many problems without seeking to rebuild the entire machinery of metropolitan governance.

APPLICATIONS TO RURAL AREAS

This volume's focus on metropolitan areas should in no way suggest that the methodology used here is less appropriate for nonmetropolitan areas.[9] Although metropolitan areas feature a greater density of governments per square mile, rural areas in fact possess many more governments per capita. If "fragmentation" is taken to mean the number of governments indexed to population, rural America has much greater fragmentation than metropolitan America. More than 60 percent of the total number of local governments in the U.S. lie outside Metropolitan Statistical Areas (MSAs). In 1987 this amounted to more than 50,000 units of local government (compared to just over 30,000 units in metropolitan areas), serving some 54.4 million people, just under 30 percent of the population. Although rural public economies have not been studied in the depth devoted to metropolitan public economies, some reasonable conjectures can be offered as to how rural areas might compare to metropolitan areas.

Descriptively, one of the distinguishing features of rural America is a relatively greater reliance on the "default" units, especially counties, 75 percent of which lie outside MSAs (compared to 61 percent of all governments). The character of rural local government is likely to vary significantly between strong-township states, located mainly in the Northeast plus Wisconsin, and strong-county states. Rural areas are also likely to differ markedly in the types of special districts that have been created. Numerous districts have been created to facilitate collective action among farmers or other users of natural resources, for example, water districts of various sorts and drainage districts. Others, in particular soil conservation districts, were created in response to national policy initiatives and therefore represent quite a different use of the special-district mechanism. Some consolidation movements have been focused on rural America—especially the consolidation of rural school districts, which have declined sharply in numbers, although some states, such as North Dakota and Nebraska, retain large numbers of small districts. In general, rural professionals have been no less accepting of consolidation as an article of faith than their metropolitan counterparts.

Despite its greater number of local governments per capita, it is likely that rural America exhibits less differentiation between provision and production. This is due to the reduced spatial density of local governments in rural areas. With fewer local governments nearby, existing governments are more likely to produce services in-house. On the provision side, low population density may be associated with a larger number of smaller distinct communities of interest. There is no reason that relatively small populations scattered across a large area should exhibit homogeneity of preferences. Even relatively small school districts, for example, may not tend to have homogeneous school populations if they are drawn from different communities located some miles apart. The result is a larger number of smaller communities of interest to be represented in the provision services and, therefore, more local governments per capita.

Rural communities clearly would encounter distinctive problems and opportunities in both the provision and production of local services. Low population density reduces demand for some local services as it increases the costs of producing other services. A relatively low demand for police services may combine with a relatively high per capita cost of producing police patrol; response times are almost certain to be higher, on average, in rural areas. Transportation costs in general are almost certain to be higher and affect the costs of production and delivery across a range of service sectors. If rural producers are unable to capture economies of scale, it is not because of jurisdictional size per se but rather because of low population density. In metropolitan areas a large number of small jurisdictions function in the context of a large public economy. In rural areas it is the size of the local public economy, not the size of particular jurisdictions, that limits the ability of producers to tap economies of scale. Neither jurisdictional nor agency consolidation offers a solution to service production problems in this context, for consolidation cannot create population scale where it is absent. Rural communities are more likely to rely on volunteer and part-time labor, as in volunteer fire departments, and on less specialized modes of production, to achieve economies in service production.

APPLICATIONS TO DEVELOPING COUNTRIES

The theory of local public economies also has application outside the U.S., especially in developing countries.[10] For at least two decades decentralization has been an emerging issue in the context of development. It has taken on added importance as democratization movements sweep through much of Africa and Latin America and as international donors increasingly stress policy reform and governance improvement as conditions and goals of development assistance. Yet the reality of decentralization is ephemeral: many if not most central governments are loath to give up real power to local actors, and even well-intentioned reform efforts fail to produce much in the way of local autonomy. The failure to achieve real decentralization has become one of the enduring puzzles of development policy.

Decentralization is sought for a set of closely related reasons. Strong local governments are thought to be the key to responsive and efficient delivery of local services, including education and medical care. Local collective action is considered essential to public problem solving in such critical policy areas as natural resource management and infrastructure maintenance. Local institutions that people can trust are viewed as a necessary condition for mobilizing fiscal resources and applying social capital to community development. Finally, local public institutions provide a training ground and platform for effective participation in national government, strengthening the capacity of citizens to defend their essential interests. For these reasons some sort of decentralization is nearly always an important dimension of the reform packages recommended for developing countries.

The widespread failure of decentralization reforms suggests the need for a fresh approach. A major part of the difficulty lies with the use of an inadequate theory and methodology for analyzing the basic problems of decentralization. Decentralizers tend to see their task as one of creating a definitive set of regional and/or local governments. This requires them to choose a uniform plan of local-government organization, which is then imposed on local communities. The alternative is to view the task of decentralization as one of creating local public economies. The key is not the creation of a discrete set of local governments but the adoption of a set of enabling rules—a local-government constitution. These are rules that enable local communities to create a variety of local-government units. Local governments directly created by central authority become "default" units—those that local communities rely upon when they choose not to create some other unit. Basic to this approach are variety—making a wide range of local-government options available for addressing diverse problems, including both general-purpose and special-purpose units of government—and freedom—allowing local communities to choose and act on their own initiative, including making their own mistakes.

A reliance on citizens to create their own units of local government is a prescription for joining local government to civic engagement. Although varying across cultures, human beings possess strong self-governing tendencies on the basis of voluntary association. Frequently, if simply left alone by the central government, local communities in developing countries assume coercive powers. But both purely voluntary association and informal local government have relatively sharp limits. The former runs into formidable free-rider problems once the size of the group increases beyond one organized on the basis of face-to-face relationships; the latter, lacking legal personality, is unable to enter into productive relationships with formal governmental units, severely restricting the scope of problems it can address. Enabling rules that let local citizens create governments allow them to resolve free-rider problems while endowing local organization with formal legal recognition. The structure of local organizations is then a product of local civic initiative and is directly tied to civil society. Local government becomes an instrument of local community, usually for addressing quite specific local problems, rather than an instrument of central authority used as a means for its own support.

In sub-Saharan Africa one of the principal problems facing development practitioners is the dichotomy between modern and indigenous governance structures. Most African societies possess two quite distinct governance structures—a formal structure associated with modern state apparatus and an informal structure associated with indigenous tribal organization. Much of the day-to-day governance of society still rests with ancient tribal institutions. Although an important source of social capital, tribal organization contributes relatively little to development because it is not integrated into the formal governance structures that are essential to development-producing activities, such as large-scale organization, the pooling of capital, and the routine enforcement of contractual obligations. Decentralization schemes frequently ignore indigenous patterns of organization, creating redundant local governance structures. When local people continue to invest themselves in institutions they have learned to trust, spurning new institutions that emanate from a source they have good reason not to trust, decentralization fails to achieve its intended purpose.

Allowing citizens to create their own local governments offers the potential for integrating modern and indigenous patterns of organization. Local communities can then draw on indigenous patterns as they create new ones that extend their previous capabilities, fashioning a local public economy that builds incrementally on existing institutions. An informal water users association, for example, can become a special-district government capable of exercising legitimate enforcement powers locally and entering into productive interorganizational arrangements regionally and nationally. In the process both formal and informal institutions can be transformed into more effective tools of development.

International donors and development practitioners who seek to assist the process of decentralization need a theory and methodology appropriate to the task. Existing patterns of organization should be studied for the contribution they can make to the organization of a local public economy both on the provision side and on the production side. Specific types of local problems should be analyzed in terms of provision and production aspects with a view to the organizational capabilities required for addressing each aspect. Enabling rules should be carefully designed to facilitate local organization that draws on existing capabilities and at the same time allows for incremental adjustments needed to address problematic situations. Over time, a constructive body of enabling rules can be assembled that allows local communities to put their own initiative and resources to best use. The ability to contribute to development in this manner is technically available today; what is lacking is a recognition of its potential, a corps of practitioners trained in its application, and the organizational will to put it to use in the right context.

PRINCIPLES OF GOVERNANCE FOR LOCAL PUBLIC ECONOMIES

If there is no "one right way" to organize a local public economy, the appropriate focus of inquiry is on governance. What is needed to guide the process of both metropolitan and nonmetropolitan organization is not a blueprint but a set of principles for designing the institutions of local governance. Based on what we know from research and supporting theory about how local public economies work, some key principles can be formulated:

- **Distinguish provision from production.**
  A lot of fuzzy thinking about local-government organization derives from the failure to distinguish provision from production. The arguments made in behalf of jurisdictional consolidation usually include benefits from large-scale production. Yet these benefits can be obtained without consolidation (often more effectively), and what is more, consolidation of provision units can make provision less responsive. *Local governments are primarily provision units.* The effects of scale on the provision side are quite different from the effects of scale on the production side of the local public economy.

- **Give citizens a broad range of options and let them choose, community by community, how to constitute their local governments.**
  Only citizens can make the trade-offs required to determine the number and variety of local governments in a metropolitan or nonmetropolitan area. Citizens need a large number of organizational options in order to fit the organization of the provision side to the spatial distribution of citizen interests and preferences. The fewer the options, the weaker the fit, and the less responsive provision will be.

  The range of alternatives should include both neighborhood and areawide provision units, plus special-purpose as well as general-purpose or multipurpose provision units; special-purpose units should include both independent and dependent districts. The following corollary principles are implied:
    - ➤ Don't consolidate jurisdictions without securing voter approval in concurrent referenda.

> ➤ Don't give special tax or intergovernmental-aid incentives to units
>   that choose to consolidate—this simply distorts the decision-making
>   process, causing it to be made on the basis of extraneous criteria.
> ➤ Don't allow local governments to annex territory without securing
>   voter approval in the area to be annexed. Unilateral annexation
>   undermines fiscal equivalence and reduces pressures for efficiency.

- **Let citizens create optional neighborhood units in large central cities or urban counties.**
  In order to obtain a more responsive mix of services that meet the test of fiscal equivalence, cities need more than a single provision unit. Once multiple provision units have been organized, new production options can also be considered. The rapid growth of Business Improvement Districts (BIDS) and similar units in urban downtowns demonstrates the inchoate demand in central cities for smaller, targeted provision units.

- **Let local officials (not central planners) decide separately how to organize production.**
  If local officials decide, new production arrangements are more apt to be truly cost-effective, that is, to actually save money. The principle includes these corollaries:
  > ➤ Let local officials decide whether to produce in-house or contract-out.
  > ➤ Let local officials decide how to organize overlying agencies designed
  >   to capture economies of scale in production.

- **Allow citizens to increase local taxes.**
  Tax limitation statutes should allow local citizens to increase taxes beyond the statutory limit by means of referenda. There is a big difference between state statutes that prevent local officials from raising revenue without citizen consent and statutes that restrict local governments regardless of citizen consent. The former empower local citizens; the latter handicap local communities.[11] Communities that require tax referenda are more apt to present citizens with tax-service packages that clarify what citizens can expect to receive from increased tax revenues.

- **Be sure that an umbrella jurisdiction overlies both central city and surrounding suburbs.**
  The umbrella jurisdiction should be a general-purpose government with its own elected officials, typically a metropolitan county. Its responsibilities should not *compete with* but instead should *complement* those of the underlying jurisdictions. An umbrella jurisdiction is not a metropolitan government—it neither controls the other jurisdictions within its boundaries nor assigns their provision and production responsibilities. Its relationship to

underlying jurisdictions is not hierarchical. Yet it will tend to define the boundaries of a metropolitan civil society and provide a convenient unit for state legislation. It will also facilitate joint action by the central city and its suburbs on common problems.

Following these governance principles, a typical metropolitan area would generate a structure of provision and production with:

- Several layers of provision, extending from neighborhood units to areawide units, with the number of layers varying from one part of the metro area to another.
- Service sectors (police, fire, schools, etc.) that include a combination of small and large production agencies organized to produce various service components.

Tying together the multiplicity of governmental jurisdictions and agencies, one can anticipate the development of a web of voluntary associations among local governments. What one should *not* expect is the simple proliferation of local governments. There is no evidence that citizens create local governments willy-nilly, without justification. Nor should one expect that small local governments would attempt, unless constrained by law or circumstances, to produce services that they are unable to produce efficiently. Ample evidence suggests the contrary.

THE RESEARCH/REFORM AGENDA

Cross-sectional research predicated on a simple dichotomy—consolidated versus fragmented metropolitan areas—will not be sufficient to advance the discussion and understanding of metropolitan organization much further. Framed as a contest between the consolidated and the fragmented, metropolitan research has a sterile future. Conducting research within these two broad categories is severely limiting. What is called fragmentation is composed of too many variables subject to too many different combinations to be lumped together in a single category. Similarly, what is called consolidation also exhibits numerous variations, many of great potential interest in a theory of local public economies. Gross comparisons between consolidated and fragmented areas contribute to the division of the metropolitan research enterprise into opposing camps more concerned with their own competition than with the advancement of knowledge and the improvement of metropolitan organization and governance.

Metropolitan governance in the United States tends to be an endogenous expression of local civil society, not an imposition by outside authorities. The rules used to govern local public economies are generated from within "civil communities," in Elazar's phrase, even when formally adopted by state legislatures. Unsatisfactory arrangements engender local efforts to change the "rules of the game." A clear distinction must be made, however, between reform proposals and the problems that give rise to them. Actual reform proposals are as much a product of the theory that people bring to their experience as of the experience itself. Experience not in conformity with an *a priori* theory can also generate efforts at reform quite apart from estimates of consequences.

The local-government constitutions used to organize the governance of metropolitan areas are subject to fairly continuous modification—tinkering at the margins of institutional arrangements. This process can hold a number of clues as to how governance relates to structure and performance. Problems are experienced; reform options, considered and assessed; incremental changes, adopted; the structure of provision or production then adjusted; and performance, finally, affected in some way. This suggests the utility of longitudinal research that focuses on practical problem solving in specific metropolitan areas. Metropolitan areas can be purposively selected for study in order to provide variation on key combinations of variables suggested by theory. The overarching question is, how do a variety of metropolitan areas address problems? More specific questions would be concerned with the extent to which particular reforms yield predicted effects.[12]

Research teams should include both scholars and practitioners. The fruitful study of specific metropolitan areas requires sophisticated *local* knowledge as well as *general* knowledge informed by theory and research. The field studies of St. Louis and Allegheny Counties conducted for the ACIR by Parks and Oakerson, although they were more in the nature of a snapshot than a longitudinal study, used a methodology that was attentive to local knowledge.[13] Their subsequent work in DuPage County, Illinois,[14] was even more intentional in an effort to incorporate local knowledge into the process of inquiry, using panels of practitioners in service sectors to collect and interpret data.

In this way the local public economy framework can be used to guide both basic and applied research. Distinguishing between the provision and production aspects of problems can clarify the criteria and information relevant to different decisions. Sorting out the pertinent governance issues from more operational issues clarifies both the level of analysis and the level of action appropriate to different aspects of a problem. Policy analysts who work within this framework can contribute to problem solving as they contribute to improved knowledge.

For research on local-government constitutions more generally, the fifty states can be used as units of analysis. This research should identify theoretically interesting rule configurations and examine their effects on the structure of local public economies. Such a research program would move beyond previous work, which has tended to examine variation in particular rules (e.g., annexation rules or home-rule provisions) with insufficient attention to how rules how configured. A central focus of this work should be on process. To what extent do governance rules frame a process that enables citizens and officials to choose appropriate provision arrangements? The study of process is essential to understand how rules affect choices. Only in this way can we learn how local public economies are governed, identify structural distortions when present, and point the way to needed reforms.

Another research effort should be focused on equity. Efficiency and equity are not unrelated, nor do they represent a simple trade-off. Provision-side efficiency may be a first-order condition for attaining equity as a second-order condition. If poor communities are deprived of the organizational means to make whatever provision they can for their collective wants, effective redistribution may not be able to occur. To shed light on this important issue, comparative research is needed between disadvantaged communities that are (1) located within large heterogeneous jurisdictions and (2) separately organized as municipalities or other autonomous jurisdictions. These differently governed communities should be compared with respect to responsiveness of service provision, self-help efforts, efficiency of production arrangements, and the productive use of intergovernmental revenues.

ALTERNATIVE FUTURES

Visions of the future American metropolis abound. David Rusk envisions a metropolis dominated by an expanding central city, a single dominant jurisdiction able to correct imbalances in growth and service provision, as well as overcome residential segregation by class and race. Anthony Downs envisions a metropolis characterized by higher density development, fewer automobiles and more subways, and more carefully planned and balanced growth between central city and suburbs. Although Downs believes that a unified metropolitan government is the preferred solution, he discards the idea as politically infeasible and focuses instead on alternative ways to achieve metropolitan-level control over land-use planning and infrastructure development. Neither Rusk nor Downs has fully assessed the costs of the solutions they propose. Understandably, policy advocates usually stress the benefit-side of the proposals they are advancing. In this case, to do otherwise would require recognizing the benefits of governmental fragmentation. When fragmentation has been declared the enemy, and is recognized as a formidable political opponent to boot, one can hardly be expected to give aid and comfort to the other side.

For most of the century, however, most scholars have been blind to the benefits of a diversified local public economy. Perhaps the blindness comes from using the wrong conceptual lenses. Different lenses are what this book has been about—an alternative way of thinking about local government in metropolitan America, one that can make sense of the distinctively American approach to local governance and one that discloses a much different metropolitan future. Examined through new lenses, the American experience with metropolitan organization and governance evokes a hopeful image of the future. The most nagging problems in metropolitan America derive, as critics allege, from the *bifurcation of the metropolis* into urban and suburban areas. In this sense, Rusk is right. But the solution is not to erase local boundaries within the metropolis, creating a monopoly provider. It is rather to extend the benefits of a diversified public economy into the central city. With the creation of BIDs, the first steps in this direction are already being taken.

The *civic metropolis* is a viable and compelling vision of the future. Its viability is well established from experience. Metropolitan civil society is no figment of the imagination. It is real and it works. The development of the civic metropolis does, however, require careful attention to its institutional architecture. Governmental institutions provide the "skeleton" that holds civil society together. Two aspects of institutional architecture are essential:

One is the institutional *infrastructure*. These are the primary units of local governance—small municipalities, school districts, RCAs, small special districts including tax districts, and now BIDs. What is essential is that small-scale communities have the capability to organize themselves to act collectively with respect to common problems. This requires that locally defined communities be able to *self-govern*, exercising the powers of government within a limited sphere—limited in terms of both territory and the scope of authority. Metropolitan areas abound with small-scale collective problems. Although some of these can be addressed through purely voluntary associations, many cannot. It is imperative that citizens have available to them instruments of collective action—of local governance—that are more accessible and readily employable than the single instrument of a large-scale metropolitan government. Collective problems require collective action, and small-scale collective problems require small-scale collective action. This same process is one that brings citizens actively into the business of local governance, engaging them in finding solutions to their common problems, rather than waiting on "the government" to solve their problems for them. Without active citizen engagement in the process of local governance, it is doubtful that any of more serious metropolitan problems can be effectively addressed. Without primary units of local governance, metropolitan organization lacks an institutional infrastructure for reaching citizens as members of local communities. One might just as well build thoroughfares without residential streets, water storage facilities without water lines, and wastewater treatment plants without connecting sewers. An urban infrastructure depends on instruments of collective action as much as on physical facilities.

The other aspect is the institutional *superstructure*. Primary units must be nested within larger units that also function as instruments of collective action on a larger scale. Default units—units that local citizens were not required to create—often can serve this purpose, for example, a county. In some metro-areas two tiers of default units prove to be useful—county and town. The larger unit acts as a *jurisdictional umbrella* that serves to define the metropolitan civil society. Civic relationships tend to develop more intensely under the umbrella than outside its reach. Very large and complex metro-areas require more than one umbrella jurisdiction, in which case some sort of still larger jurisdiction—most likely a special-purpose government—may be useful. What is most important is to establish an umbrella jurisdiction that overlies both the central city and its surrounding suburban municipalities—at least out to some territorial limit. City-county separation is one of the more destructive legacies of an earlier period of metro-reform, for it bifurcates not only the governmental structure of the metro-area but also the metropolitan civil society, setting up a superstructure more conducive to city-county rivalry and cooperation. Although an umbrella jurisdiction should be a general-purpose government, it should not be competitive with the local municipalities within its boundaries. Its functions should be complementary to more local functions rather than substitutive. This does not imply, however, an absence of conflict between large-scale and small-scale concerns. This sort of conflict is inevitable and is one of the reasons that a strong metropolitan civil society is needed. Conflict resolution is a principal dimension of metropolitan governance. Neither should conflict be suppressed, for important values may be at stake on all sides of an issue. Neighborhood values and regional values are deserving of equal representation at the table of metropolitan organization.

The institutional architecture of metropolitan governance needs to facilitate collective problem solving at multiple levels of organization. Both highly localized and regional problems require collective action at an appropriate scale. When conflicts emerge between levels, there need to be arrangements for resolving those conflicts constructively. Solutions to regional problems, while they may require regional action, cannot be allowed to dominate more local concerns. Strong proponents of metropolitan governments usually are strongly focused on some set of regional problems—suburban sprawl, transit, redevelopment, racial integration, and fiscal equity. These are of course legitimate problems, a cause for serious concern. But solutions need to be *carefully crafted* to fit the problems being addressed; otherwise, important institutional capabilities may be thoughtlessly destroyed in the process. Regional problems, however serious, should be addressed in ways that respect other, equally important, capabilities for collective action at more local levels. In some cases, regional problem solving may entail creating new regional institutions or assigning new regional powers to existing institutions. What Downs views as a second-best approach to regional problems is from this perspective the preferred *modus operandi*. The superstructure of metropolitan organization must not be allowed to devour its institutional infrastructure. If this happens, one of the principal casualties will be problem solving—at all levels.

CONCLUSION

The civic metropolis is not a vision of an ideal metropolitan world. Ideal worlds exist only in a human imagination that neglects some essential values and the required trade-offs among them. The civic metropolis is nevertheless a possible world that holds considerable promise for making the required trade-offs in ways that do not neglect essential values. The American system of local government rests on republican principles of local self-governance. These principles serve essential democratic values: the consent of the governed, strong representation, local liberty, community, and active citizenship. Some of the most thoughtful reflections on American politics at the end of the century have concluded that these are precisely the values that now need to be strengthened, if the American political tradition is to survive and prosper. Now is no time to weaken those values further still for the next generation of Americans by depriving many, if not most, of them of *truly local* governments. Nor is it necessary to do so in order to address even the most pressing metropolitan problems.

However, the civic metropolis is not simply self-generating. It depends on an institutional architecture informed by an analysis of local public economies and continuously subject to adjustment through reform. Scholars have essential contributions to make to a new and more constructive agenda of metropolitan reform, just as practitioners have important contributions to make to metropolitan scholarship. The imperative for both scholar and practitioner is to avoid the tempting trap of partisan advocacy in behalf of extreme solutions to specific problems. Perhaps the threat of metropolitan government is useful rhetorically for getting the attention of the more shortsighted and comfortable members of the metropolitan community. The risk lies with the politician who believes his or her own rhetoric. Citizens do not want a "metropolitan revolution," and they will not tolerate it simply because reformers fail to appreciate the values they inadvertently threaten. The civic metropolis is hard work—not only for the citizens engaged in it but also for scholars who would study it and reformers who would increase its productivity.

The study of metropolitan organization demands a framework that can address the variety of provision, production, and governance problems that occur in the metropolitan context. Articulating such a framework was the basic task set for this book, alongside reviewing the more relevant research. Implicit in the framework is a conception of the metropolis as a civic creation. This aspect of the framework is presuppositional. It does not derive from empirical data, though it does not contradict the data. It arises instead from the rich tradition of American local self-government, rooted in the republicanism of the founding generation, observed and expounded by Alexis de Tocqueville, and developed by generations of Americans who built more than 83,000 units of local government. This was and continues to be a great work of citizenship, leaving a valuable cultural inheritance for addressing present and future generations of problems.

APPENDIX A

COMMISSION FINDINGS AND CONCLUSIONS

U.S. Advisory Commission on Intergovernmental Relations, *The Organization of Local Public Economies*

T HE COMMISSION FINDS THAT the nation needs as its local foundation the most efficient and responsive—dynamic and creative—local public economies possible. It is a necessary foundation, not only for an efficient and responsive national public economy, but also for promoting greater equity through intergovernmental sharing. The efficient and responsive performance of local public economies—the complex of public and private organizations that supply local public goods and services in American communities—has depended historically upon rules that allow a variety of local units to emerge from a process of citizen choice.

The Commission concludes that the following general principles are useful in guiding the organization of local self-government in the American federal system:

1. VARIETY AND DIVERSITY

A strong case can be made for local governments that range in size from small neighborhood units to areawide units and, in functional scope, from single-purpose to multipurpose units. To obtain the benefits of large-scale organization, it is unnecessary and unwise to drive out small-scale organization. Large and small, as well as single-purpose and multipurpose, units of local government, when used concurrently, reflect complementary expressions of public preference, not contradictory principles of organization.

From ACIR, *The Organization of Local Public Economies*, Rept. A–109, December 1987, 53–54.

2. DISTINGUISHING PROVISION AND PRODUCTION

Local governments can usefully be viewed as "provision units," organizations that make provision—both through tax and spending decisions and regulations—for local public goods and services. As provision units, local governments can choose how to carry out "production," whether by organizing their own production units through government departments, or by contracting out to private firms or other governmental agencies. The ability to make this choice is a basic principle of local governance.

3. OPPORTUNITIES FOR INITIATIVE, CREATIVITY, AND COOPERATION

The efficiency and productivity of local public economies depends upon opportunities for initiative, creativity, cooperation, and public entrepreneurship. These opportunities are associated with both the potential variety in provision arrangements available to local citizens and the development of alternative ways of relating provision to production, including both government production and private contracting. Distinguishing provision and production allows for greater variety in both. A significant reduction in the number and variety of local government units, in order to unite provision and production, could actually reduce the opportunities available to local citizens and officials to increase efficiency and productivity.

4. CITIZEN CHOICE AND CONSENT IN LOCAL GOVERNANCE

The governance of local public economies—"metropolitan" governance in an urban/suburban context—is best viewed as a problem in defining and altering the basic "rules of the game." These rules—usually in the formal province of state legislatures—concern the formation of local government units, boundary changes (such as annexation), revenue raising and regulatory capabilities, and interjurisdictional relationships (cooperation and contracting). The unity of a metropolitan or rural community depends upon the coherence of these basic rules of local governance, and upon an underlying consensus, not upon the creation of a single dominant unit of local government or upon any detailed blueprint for local government reorganization. The particular pattern of local government units in a community emerges, over time, from the choices that citizens and officials make within the basic rules of local governance.

Rules that allow citizens to make the basic structural and fiscal decisions pertaining to local governance are more likely to yield results consistent with citizen preferences. Local citizens, historically, are the creators and sustainers of American local government. Citizens are also "coproducers" of public services alongside of government officials. They are not simply the consumers of local services supplied in jurisdictions created by others.

5. EQUITY AND COMMUNITY CHOICE

Standards of equity in the distribution of local public goods and services are a fundamental consideration along with standards of efficiency. The quest for greater equity, however, cannot effectively be pursued independently of the search for efficiency, productivity, and responsiveness. To seek equity in ways that subtract significantly from the efficiency and productivity of a local public economy is to redistribute a shrinking economic pie. To seek equity in ways that subtract significantly from the responsiveness of service provision is to undermine citizen choice and consent.

Equity considerations alone may be insufficient to justify a reduction in the number and variety of provision units in a local public economy. At the same time, equity concerns can be, and ought to be, vigorously addressed by overlapping jurisdictions, metropolitan as well as state and national. Interjurisdictional fiscal transfers and local tax-base sharing may be more effective instruments for addressing equity concerns in the context of continued efficiency and responsiveness than expanded local government boundaries intended solely to create the possibility of intrajurisdictional transfers.

In addressing equity concerns, citizen choice and consent remain important principles. A highly efficient and responsive local public economy is better able to address the problems of distressed communities and is likely to offer better stewardship of funds received from both state and national governments. Greater equity depends upon both self-reliance and a willingness to share. Citizens in distressed communities may be especially needful of autonomous community organization, so as to be able to receive intergovernmental funding and use it to local community advantage.

6. STATE LEGISLATURES: TRUSTEES
OF LOCAL GOVERNANCE

State legislatures are the trustees of the basic rules of local governance in America. The laws and constitutions of each state are the basic legal instruments of local governance. Legislatures must, by distinguishing provision and production, understand the need for variety and diversity. They should also understand that responsive local governance depends upon opportunities for citizen choice and a need to obtain citizen consent. Where there is little variety on the provision side—as in many large central cities—legis-latures have the authority to create new potential for variety by enabling neighborhoods to incorporate, and should do so. Where there is little citizen choice and little separation of provision from production, state leg-islatures should closely examine the basic rules of local governance in order to open up new possibilities, and allow a more creative and efficient local public economy to emerge from the choices of local citizens and their elected officials.

APPENDIX B
COMMISSION RECOMMENDATIONS

U.S. Advisory Commission on Intergovernmental Relations,
The Organization of Local Public Economies

Recommendation 1:
NONVIABLE GOVERNMENTS

The Commission rescinds its 1981 recommendation on the dissolution of "nonviable governments." The 1981 recommendation is quoted in full below:

> The Commission recommends that states, through a local government boundary commission, other state agency, or the state legislature, establish or supplement standards for local government viability (a) by requiring any local government, general or special-purpose, in the urbanized portion of a standard metropolitan statistical area (SMSA), to have the equivalent of at least one full-time employee, or, (b) by requiring general-purpose units to perform at least four functions, or only two functions, provided that each of the two constitutes at least 10% of the jurisdiction's current expenditure budget. If either of these standards is not met, the state, after offering adequate opportunity for a hearing for the affected local government(s), shall consider dissolving the local government and providing for the transfer to and performance of its functions by (an) appropriate unit(s) of general local government. [*State and Local Roles in the Federal System*, A–88, April 1982, 446–47]

From ACIR, *The Organization of Local Public Economies*, Rept. A–109, December 1987, 55–56. Recommendations adopted unanimously by the Commission on June 5, 1987 in San Francisco, California.

The Commission concludes that, while the viability of units of local government is an important issue, criteria pertaining to the number of full-time equivalent employees and the number of functions produced rather than provided are inappropriate standards for determining local government viability. Small units of government that make use of part-time citizen-officials and that function as "pure provision" units, contracting for the production of most or even all services provided, may serve very useful purposes for their citizens. Lack of viability as a production unit does not necessarily indicate lack of viability as a provision unit.

Different criteria apply to organizing the *provision* of local public goods and services as distinguished from their *production*. The provision side involves financing, specifying performance standards, and representing the interests of citizen-consumers. The production side is concerned with making a product or delivering a service. Very small units of local government (under 1,000 in population) can serve useful purposes on the provision side, even when they do not function as production units. The ACIR study of St. Louis County, where twenty-one municipalities under 1,000 population are located, demonstrates the viability of very small units as organizations for the provision of services, while production is contracted to a variety of public agencies and private firms.

Small suburban municipalities, despite their legal status, tend to function effectively as "neighborhood governments," a concept endorsed by the Commission as recently as 1985. No evidence exists to support the view that small units necessarily impede the performance of areawide functions where those functions are assigned to an overlapping jurisdiction. To dissolve these local units of government without the consent of their citizens would violate both the democratic process and the historic tradition of American local self-governance.

Recommendation 2:
SPECIAL-PURPOSE GOVERNMENTS

The Commission finds that special-purpose governments may be a useful and efficient form of organization for local citizens. The option of organizing a special-purpose government complements the organization of general-purpose local governments. The Commission finds no a priori reason to reduce the number of special-purpose governments or to restrict their growth arbitrarily. The utility of special-purpose governments is best judged on a case-by-case basis.

The Commission recommends, therefore, that states place no extra-ordinary limits or procedural burdens upon the creation of special-purpose governments by local citizens.

The utility of special-purpose governments derives from the inherent limitations of general-purpose governments. Municipalities tend to be mutually exclusive jurisdictions; their boundaries generally cannot overlap. Counties and townships may overlap municipalities, but have relatively fixed boundaries. Special-purpose governments have flexible boundaries and may overlap other units, including municipalities. The use of special-purpose governments enables local communities to obtain a closer match between the geographical scope of problems and the jurisdictional boundaries of a unit of local government organized to address those problems. Special-purpose governments also address the needs of citizens who desire only a limited range of services.

Recommendation 3:
BOUNDARY REVIEW AGENCIES

The Commission finds that many of the reasons that once supported the idea that states ought to create either state or local boundary review agencies have been brought into serious question, both by events and by new research. The Commission recommends, therefore, that caution be exercised in the establishment and use of boundary review agencies, especially those empowered to veto the creation of local units of government by affected citizens.

Boundary review agencies are created for the purpose of regulating the establishment of new units of local government, as well as controlling boundary adjustments through annexation and consolidation. The premise often is that local citizens are not competent to make appropriate judgments about local government organization. Distinguishing provision units from production units, and recognizing that local governments are fundamentally provision units, suggests that local citizens may in fact be "the experts" on the number and variety of local government jurisdictions that ought to exist in a local area. Boundary review agencies ought not to be used by local government officials to stifle citizen initiative and forestall competitive pressures for efficient local government performance. The ability to create new units of local government, and give their consent to an expansion in the boundaries of existing units, are important citizen capabilities in the organization of local public economies.

NOTES

CHAPTER ONE: THE STUDY OF LOCAL PUBLIC ECONOMIES

1. For a useful summary of the new institutionalism see Thráinn Eggertsson, *Economic Behavior and Institutions* (New York: Cambridge University Press, 1990). The most comprehensive application of institutionalist thought to American local government is Vincent Ostrom, Robert Bish, and Elinor Ostrom, *Local Government in the United States* (Oakland, Calif.: ICS Press, 1988). Earlier efforts include Robert L. Bish, *The Public Economy of Metropolitan Areas* (Chicago: Markham Publishing Co., 1971), and Robert L. Bish and Vincent Ostrom, *Understanding Urban Government: Metropolitan Reform Reconsidered* (Washington, D.C.: American Enterprise Institute, 1973).

2. See, for example, Paul E. Peterson, *City Limits* (Chicago: University of Chicago Press, 1981).

3. See especially volume 1, chapter 5. Randy Hamilton makes a similar point in "Self-Government through Citizen Legislators: The Bedrock of Liberty" in ACIR, *Is Constitutional Reform Necessary to Reinvigorate Federalism? A Roundtable Discussion*, M–154, November 1987.

4. See Vincent Ostrom, *The Meaning of Democracy and the Vulnerability of Democracies* (Ann Arbor: The University of Michigan Press, 1997).

5. Richard A. Musgrave, *The Theory of Public Finance: A Study in Public Economy* (New York: McGraw-Hill Book Company, 1959), 15.

6. Vincent Ostrom, Charles M. Tiebout, and Robert Warren, "The Organization of Government in Metropolitan Areas: A Theoretical Inquiry," *American Political Science Review* 55 (December 1961): 838. Reprinted in Vincent Ostrom, *The Meaning of American Federalism* (Oakland, Calif.: ICS Press, 1991), 137–161.

7. This account of the distinction between provision and production is based in part on the discussion found in Vincent Ostrom and Elinor Ostrom, "Public Goods and Public Choices," in Vincent Ostrom, *The Meaning of American Federalism* (Oakland, Calif.: ICS Press, 1991), 163–197. The distinction between provision and production has also been elaborated by Ted Kolderie, "Rethinking Public Service Delivery" in *The Entrepreneur in Local Government*, ed. Barbara H. Moore (Washington, D.C.: International City

139

Management Association, 1983), 43–48. Also see Kolderie, "The Two Concepts of Privatization," *Public Administration Review* 46 (July/August 1986): 285–291.

8. Provision thus consists of a wide range of decisions and activities. The focus in this discussion is on the public provision of goods and services and the activities associated with this type of provisioning. This is not to negate the importance of other provision choices, including the choice of nonprovision or privatization; rather, it is to examine one important dimension of local provision activity in depth and to trace the implications of various organizational choices for the structure of local public economies.

9. See Gordon P. Whitaker, "Coproduction: Citizen Participation in Service Delivery," *Public Administration Review* 40 (May/June 1980): 240–246.

10. See the discussion of residential community associations (RCAs) in chapter 3.

11. Royce Hanson, "The Urban Future: New Policies and Issues," *Journal of Housing* 44 (January/February 1987): 18.

12. A large literature exists on problems of majority voting. Two of the basic sources are Kenneth J. Arrow, *Social Choice and Individual Values*, rev. ed. (New York: John Wiley and Sons, 1963) and Duncan Black, *The Theory of Committees and Elections* (Cambridge: Cambridge University Press, 1958).

13. Technically, economists have found that majority decisions tend to reflect the preference of the median voter in a majority decision process as long as the distribution of preferences is unimodal. The greater the heterogeneity of preferences, the greater the percentage of people likely to be relatively unsatisfied with median-level provision.

14. Robert A. Dahl, *After the Revolution*, rev. ed. (New Haven: Yale University Press, 1990.)

15. Mancur Olson, "The Principle of 'Fiscal Equivalence': The Division of Responsibility among Different Levels of Government," *American Economic Review* 59 (May 1969): 479–487.

16. See Bruce W. Hamilton, "A Review: Is the Property Tax a Benefit Tax?" in *Local Provision of Public Services: The Tiebout Model after Twenty-Five Years*, ed. George R. Zodrow (New York: Academic Press, 1983). For an alternative point of view, see George R. Zodrow and Peter Mieszkowski, "The Incidence of the Property Tax: The Benefit View versus the New View," in the same volume.

17. The criterion of preference revelation does suggest a minimum size constraint for provision units as determined by the scale of specific problems. This criterion alone would limit the proliferation of small units; otherwise, the principle of fiscal equivalence would lead toward the organization of a separate municipality for every household.

18. The costs of organization and operation are construed as transaction costs, in the main, because the discussion here pertains exclusively to the provision side. While it is true that some of the costs of setting up a provision unit will involve capital costs (e.g., building and maintaining a city hall) and labor costs (e.g., paying a city manager), most of the capital and labor costs of local government pertain to production, not provision. In general, provision-side costs are best viewed as transaction costs—the costs of individual and joint decision making involved in sustaining social relationships. Some labor costs can be viewed as specialized transaction costs, analogous to the cost of hiring a lawyer or a negotiator in the private sector, incurred in representing the interests of individuals and groups to others. For a general discussion of transaction costs, see Oliver E. Williamson, "Transaction-Cost Economics: The Governance of Contractual Relations," *Journal of Law and Economics* 22 (October 1979): 223–261.

19. David L. Chicoine and Norman Walzer estimate the *average cost* of financial control for one additional governmental unit per 1000 residents in Illinois at $1.21 per capita. For an additional special district the cost is estimated to be $2.03 per capita. Chicoine and Walzer interpret these findings as "consistent with the commonly held view of duplication." Whether such "duplication" is wasteful, however, depends upon how citizens evaluate the benefit side of an additional unit. Chicoine and Walzer, *Governmental Structure and Local Public Finance* (Boston: Oelgeschlager, Gunn & Hain, 1985), 223.

20. See chapter 5 for a discussion of these rules.

21. Examples of both can be found in the ACIR study of St. Louis County. Forty percent of the county population remains unincorporated. Although incorporation movements have begun in some parts of the county in response to changing preference patterns, other parts of the county, although recognized as communities for many years, have not chosen to incorporate. Moreover, a few small municipalities have chosen to consolidate. See ACIR, *Metropolitan Organization: The St. Louis Case*, 1988.

22. The technical term is "production function," a specification of how various combinations of inputs can be transformed into outputs through the application of available technologies. See Werner Z. Hirsch, *Urban Economic Analysis* (New York: McGraw-Hill, 1973). The production functions of many local public goods and services are not known.

23. Part of the information needed to make sound production decisions has to be specific as to time and place. General knowledge is insufficient. For example, in street services one has to know when a pothole develops and where it is located in order to patch it. Similarly, in police services the ability to distinguish strangers from residents, or the unusual occurrence from the commonplace, depends on having community-specific knowledge.

24. See Roger B. Parks, et al., "Consumers as Coproducers of Public Services: Some Economic and Political Considerations," *Policy Studies Journal* 9 (summer 1981): 1,001–1,011 and Gordon P. Whitaker, "Coproduction: Citizen Participation in Service Delivery," *Public Administration Review* 40 (May/June 1980): 240–246.

25. The most thorough discussion of economies of scale in the public sector is found in the work of Hirsch, op. cit., 331–334. In general, these economies are described by a U-shaped relationship to the size of local jurisdictions with constant returns to scale over a very wide range. For labor intensive services, such as police patrol, economies of scale are exhausted very quickly, perhaps by a community as small as 4,000 people. This refers to the actual patrol component, however, and not to support services, such as radio communications.

26. Ibid.

27. This subject is developed more fully in chapter 4.

28. See Roger B. Parks and Ronald J. Oakerson, "Metropolitan Organization and Governance: A Local Public Economy Approach," *Urban Affairs Quarterly* 25, no. 1 (September 1989): 18–29.

29. Not all of the important implications are explored in this volume. Neither regulatory activity on the provision side, nor franchising and vouchering as important options for linking provision to production, are further developed here. Instead, the remainder of the discussion is focused on implications for service provision and production, examined from both efficiency and equity standpoints.

CHAPTER TWO: SEPARATING PROVISION AND PRODUCTION

1. ACIR, *Intergovernmental Service Arrangements for Delivering Local Public Services: Update 1983*, A–103, October 1985, 45–53.

2. Thomas Borcherding, Werner Pommerehne, and Friedrich Schneider, "Comparing the Efficiency of Private and Public Sector Arrangements," *Journal of Law and Economics*, Supplement 2 (1982): 127–156.

3. Louis De Alessi, "An Economic Analysis of Government Ownership and Regulation: Theory and Evidence from the Electric Power Industry," *Public Choice* 19 (1974): 1–42, and Robert W. Spann, "Public Versus Private Provision of Government Services," in *Budgets and Bureaucrats: The Sources of Government Growth*, ed. Thomas Borcherding (Durham, N.C.: Duke University Press, 1977), 71–89.

4. Roger S. Ahlbrandt, Jr., "Efficiency in the Provision of Fire Services," *Public Choice* 18 (1973): 1–15.

5. Stephen L. Mehay, "Intergovernmental Contracting for Police Services: An Empirical Analysis," *Land Economics* 55 (1979): 59–72. See also, for somewhat mixed results, Sidney Sonenblum, John J. Kirlin, and John C. Ries, *How Cities Provide Services: An Evaluation of Alternative Delivery Structures* (Cambridge, Mass.: Ballinger Publishing Co., 1977), chapter 5.

6. Robert T. Deacon, "State and Local Expenditure," in *Essays in Public Finance and Financial Management: State and Local Perspectives*, eds. John E. Peterson and C. L. Spain (New York: Chatham House, 1978), 22–33, and Borcherding, Pommerehne, and Schneider, op. cit.

7. See Barbara Stevens, *Delivery of Municipal Services Efficiently*, U.S. Department of Housing and Urban Development, 1982.

8. Martin and Stein studied the experience of American local governments with respect to contracting in the early 1980s. For this purpose, data on municipal contracting was collected from two separate surveys of municipal governments for the period 1982–1983. The International City Management Association conducted both surveys. The samples for both surveys were selected from the same "universe" of communities: all cities with populations over 10,000 and a one-eighth sample by geographical region of cities with populations under 10,000. The 1982 study surveyed local governmental units about their use of private sector service contracts for sixty-four functional activities. The 1983 study queried a comparable sample of governments on their use of intergovernmental and joint service agreements for the provision of forty-two functional activities. Data from both surveys were merged producing a sample of 890 communities that responded to both surveys. The merged data set provides information on intergovernmental and private (profit and nonprofit) service contracts for thirty-four functions in seven functional areas. The distribution of cases for the merged sample on measures of region location, population size, form of government and metropolitan status show them to be representative of the total "population" of all cities over 10,000 in the United States. The sample of cities under 10,000 is too small (only seventeen observations) to allow any meaningful generalizations about this class of cities. The complete data analysis is contained in Stein and Martin, "Contracting for Municipal Services," ACIR Technical Paper, 1987. The reader may want to compare the findings discussed here with an analysis by James M. Ferris, "The Decision to Contract Out: An Empirical Analysis," *Urban Affairs Quarterly* 22 (December 1986): 289–311. See also James M. Ferris and Elizabeth Grady, "Contracting Out: For What? With Whom?" *Public Administration Review* 46 (July/August 1986): 332–344.

9. This finding is not borne out in the analysis done by Ferris, op. cit.

10. This finding emerges only from a multivariate analysis that controls for other factors affecting the level of contracting. A large number of small governments are found in nonmetropolitan areas where potential competition among vendors would be lower.

11. See ACIR, *Metropolitan Organization: The St. Louis Case*, 1988.

12. Another provision-arrangement variable that is significant in table 2.1 is the choice of a city-manager form of government. This finding should be treated with some caution, however, since other analysts have not substantiated it. Ferris, op. cit., finds no relationship between city manager form and extent of contracting.

13. ACIR Technical Paper, 1987.

14. Stevens, op. cit., found that some self-producing cities performed specific functions more efficiently, taking account of service quality, than contracting cities, even though the pronounced tendency was for more efficient performance by contracting cities.

15. Sonenblum, Kirlin, and Rees, op. cit.

16. Ibid.

17. ACIR, *State Aid to Local Government*, A–34, April 1969, 25–27.

18. ACIR, *State and Local Roles in the Federal System*, A–88, April 1982, 446–448.

19. See Appendix, Recommendation One.

20. See *Metropolitan Organization: The St. Louis Case*, 1988.

21. See Robert O. Warren, *Government in Metropolitan Regions* (Davis: Institute of Governmental Affairs, University of California, 1966).

22. Anthony Downs, *Urban Problems and Prospects*, 2d ed. (Chicago: Rand McNally College Publishing Company, 1976), chapter 12.

23. The prevalence of contracting-out among both very large and very small municipalities—its lower incidence among midsize municipalities—suggests the possibility of an optimal municipal size in the middle range. This conclusion presumes, however, that contracting is an inferior alternative, one to be minimized—a dubious proposition empirically. It also presumes that provision-side organization should be driven by production-side criteria—that citizens do not benefit as consumers from variety in the scale of municipal organization.

24. Officials in pure provision units can conceivably exhibit a "provision bias," i.e., a bias in favor of providing, as opposed to not providing, services.

CHAPTER THREE: ORGANIZING THE PROVISION SIDE

1. See Ronald J. Oakerson and Roger B. Parks, "Local Government constitutions: A Different View of Metropolitan Governance" in *The American Review of Public Administration* 19, no. 4 (December 1989): 279–294.

2. The size of the default unit is particularly important in rural areas, where low population densities make municipal organization less attractive. Township-organized states have quite different systems of rural public organization than county-organized states. See Ronald J. Oakerson, "Structures and Patterns of Rural Governance," in *The Changing American Countryside: Rural People and Places*, ed. Emery N. Castle (Lawrence, Kansas: University Press of Kansas, 1995), 397–418.

3. In New England, "towns" are organized much like townships, but tend to function as municipalities.

4. In Virginia, counties and municipalities have separate jurisdictions. The same is also true in special cases, such as the separation of St. Louis City from St. Louis County and Baltimore City from Baltimore County.

5. ACIR, *The Problem of Special Districts in American Government*, A–22, May 1964, 73–84.

6. See ACIR Recommendation 2 printed in the Appendix.

7. Donald Foster Stetzer, *Special Districts in Cook County: Toward a Geography of Local Government*, Research Paper No. 169 (Chicago: The University of Chicago, Department of Geography, 1975).

8. Robert B. Hawkins, Jr., *Self-Government by District: Myth and Reality* (Stanford: Hoover Institution Press, 1976), 116.

9. Some independent districts that overlie smaller municipalities might be better organized as dependent districts or joint production units. For example, fire protection districts that serve the residents of small municipalities need not be organized as independent districts. Indeed, the organization of an independent district for fire protection tends to privilege fire protection in comparison with other municipal services, allowing a fire protection board direct access to the local property tax base. Critics of special districts often focus on this privileging of access to revenue-sources as a defect of the institution. Sometimes, of course, privileged access is exactly what district framers wish to create. When citizens directly control property tax rates through referenda, privileged access may not be as problematic. Nonetheless, this is an issue that local citizens and officials should be sure to consider as they debate the merits and demerits of alternative institutional arrangements.

10. On the organization of groundwater see William Blomquist, *Dividing the Waters: Governing Groundwater in South California* (Oakland, Calif.: ICS Press, 1992). A broader discussion can be found in ACIR, *Coordinating Water Resources in the Federal System: The Groundwater-Surface Water Connection*, 1991. For an earlier discussion of special districts see John C. Bollens, *Special District Government in the United States* (Berkeley: University of California Press, 1957).

11. For an engaging and instructive account of the use of special districts for such a purpose in California, see Blomquist, op. cit.

12. David L. Chicoine and Norman Walzer, *Governmental Structure and Local Public Finance* (Boston: Oelgeschlager, Gunn & Hain, 1985), 80. One possible difficulty with this finding is that home-rule authority is automatically extended to municipalities larger than 25,000 population, but to others only by local referendum. Thus, to some extent, a negative correlation between the percentage of citizens living in home-rule municipalities and number of governments per 10,000 citizens may be expected.

13. This was apparently accomplished in Illinois when the Illinois Constitution of 1970 extended fiscal home-rule to municipalities.

14. New York State Legislative Commission on State-Local Relations, *New York's State-Local Service Delivery System* (Albany, N.Y.: May 1987), 314.

15. It should also be noted that informed critics of special-purpose districts do not object—at least not as strenuously—to dependent districts. However, similar objections are often made to the use of earmarked revenues, which restrict the discretion of the taxing/budgeting authority.

16. *The Political Economy of Special Purpose Government* (Washington, D.C.: Georgetown University Press, 1997).

17. Howard Frant makes a similar point in "High-Powered and Low-Powered Incentives in the Public Sector," *JPART* 6, no. 3 (1996): 365–81, arguing that special-district managers can take a long-term view and more easily make infrastructure reinvestments.

18. Residential community associations (RCAs) include condominiums and housing cooperatives as well as homeowners associations. ACIR sponsored the study and discussion of this phenomenon in 1988–89 and published two reports: (1) *Residential Community Associations: Private Governments in the Intergovernmental System?* (1989), a collection of essays by leading scholars, and (2) *Residential Community Associations: Questions and Answers for Public Officials* (1989). For an updated, thorough treatment, see Robert Jay Dilger, *Neighborhood Politics: Residential Community Associations in American Governance* (New York: New York University Press, 1992).

19. See a study published by the Joint Economic Committee of Congress, "Stimulating Community Enterprise: A Response to Fiscal Strains in the Public Sector," December 31, 1984.

20. See Ronald J. Oakerson, "Analyzing the Commons: A Framework," in *Making the Commons Work*, ed. Daniel W. Bromley (Oakland, Calif.: ICS Press, 1992), 41–59. The Bromley volume contains a number of useful case studies of common-property organization, all concerned, however, with natural resources.

21. Although an ACIR study was unable to generate a complete census of subdivisions in the county, twenty-seven municipalities reported a total of 427 street-providing subdivisions. See ACIR, *Metropolitan Organization: The St. Louis Case*, 1988.

22. With rare exceptions, these subdivisions are "pure provision" units. All services are contracted out either to private or public vendors.

23. Many RCAs, especially those created over the last twenty years, include highly restrictive covenants, regulating the residential use of property in much greater detail than the typical zoning ordinance. Some—so-called gated communities—also attempt to control entry and exit. Both trends are problematic and reflect the private-law basis of RCA formation. Neighborhood governments created pursuant to state law could more readily be precluded from engaging in the more intrusive and exclusionary practices.

24. Jane Jacobs, *The Death and Life of Great American Cities* (New York: Vintage Books, 1961). See especially chapters 2–4.

25. See Elinor Ostrom, *Governing the Commons* (Cambridge: Cambridge University Press, 1990).

26. See Paul Peterson, *City Limits* (Chicago: University of Chicago Press, 1981).

27. See Jaesong Choe, *The Organization of Urban Common-Property Institutions: The Case of Apartment Communities in Seoul*, Ph.D. dissertation, Indiana University, December 1992.

28. For an overview see Janet Rothenberg Pack, "BIDs, DIDs, SIDs, SADs: Private Governments in America," *The Brookings Review* 10, no. 4 (Fall 1992): 18–21.

29. Russell M. Silipigni, "BID! The New Kid in Town," unpublished paper, Department of History and Political Science, Houghton College, Houghton, New York.

30. Some BIDs may also have incentives to exclude persons viewed as "undesirable" from using the public spaces in their business districts. Aggressive surveillance can threaten the rights of citizens to make lawful use of public spaces, whether the monitors are BID-employees or city police.

31. There is an extensive literature on the perverse incentives of unanimity rules under definable circumstances. For a general discussion, see James M. Buchanan and

Gordon Tullock, *The Calculus of Consent* (Ann Arbor: The University of Michigan Press, 1962).

32. Two books have become classic statements on this subject: Milton Kotler, *Neighborhood Government: The Local Foundations of Political Life* (Indianapolis: Bobbs-Merrill, 1969) and Alan Altshuler, *Community Control: The Black Demand for Participation in Large American Cities* (New York: Pegasus, 1970).

33. ACIR, *Fiscal Balance in the American Federal System*, vol. 2, Metropolitan Fiscal Disparities, A–31, October 1967, 16–17.

34. ACIR, *The States and Distressed Communities: The Final Report*, A–101, November 1985, 245.

35. More research on the prospects and pitfalls of neighborhood incorporation is needed. Experience with neighborhood advisory commissions and voluntary neighborhood associations in large central cities can usefully be compared to small municipalities and organized subdivisions in metropolitan counties. The experience of neighborhood development corporations can also be examined for possible lessons in organization.

36. See ACIR, *Metropolitan Organization: The St. Louis Case*, 1987.

37. A useful summary of much of this research program can be found in Elinor Ostrom, "Size and Performance in a Federal System," *Publius* 6 (spring 1976): 33–73. Also see Elinor Ostrom and Gordon P. Whitaker, "Does Local Community Control of Police Make a Difference? Some Preliminary Findings, *American Journal of Political Science* 17 (February 1973): 48–76; Elinor Ostrom and Roger B. Parks, "Suburban Police Departments: Too Many and Too Small?" in *The Urbanization of the Suburbs: Urban Affairs Annual Reviews* 7, eds. Louis H. Masotti and Jeffrey K. Hadden (Beverly Hills: Sage Publications, 1973), 303–402; and Elinor Ostrom and Gordon P. Whitaker, "Community Control and Governmental Responsiveness: The Case of Police in Black Neighborhoods," in *Urban Policy Analysis: Directions for Future Research: Urban Affairs Annual Reviews* 8, ed. Terry N. Clark (Beverly Hills: Sage Publications, 1974), 303–334.

38. Herbert Kiesling, "Measuring a Local Government Service: A Study of School Districts in New York State," *Review of Economics and Statistics* 49 (August 1967): 356–367.

39. William Niskanen and Mickey Levy, "Cities and Schools: A Case for Community Government in California," Working Paper No. 14 (Berkeley: Graduate School of Public Policy, University of California, 1974).

40. The procedure used was two-stage least squares regression.

41. DuPage Intergovernmental Task Force, *Inside DuPage County: Structure and Performance*, September 1992.

42. Integrated provision by the smaller unit is also a possibility, but economies of scale in the production of treatment means that the smaller unit would have to buy treatment services from a regional producer. The lack of adequate municipal incentive to maintain sewer lines can be addressed by measuring the flow received from each municipality and charging each municipality accordingly. In this event, the local provider fully internalizes the costs of both collection and treatment. The measurement of wastewater flow, however, is often held to be inaccurate.

43. Richard E. Wagner and Warren E. Weber, "Competition, Monopoly, and the Organization of Government in Metropolitan Areas," *Journal of Law and Economics* 18 (December 1975): 661–684.

44. Thomas Dilorenzo, "Economic Competition and Political Competition: An Empirical Note," *Public Choice* 40 (1983): 203–209.

45. Mark Schneider, "Fragmentation and the Growth of Government," *Public Choice* 48 (1986): 255–263.

46. It should be noted that Chicoine and Walzer did not replicate these findings in a study limited to 101 Illinois counties, excluding Cook County. Using traditional measures of fragmentation, they found no relationship to expenditures. They also found a positive relationship to expenditures using an indicator of fragmentation based upon industrial organization theory; they did not, however, provide a replication of Dilorenzo's industrial concentration model. Chicoine and Walzer also argue that special districts have been created in Illinois as a response to fiscal limits on general-purpose local governments. If this is the case, the number of governmental units may in fact be suboptimal; that is, there may be too many governments in this case.

47. Ostrom and Parks, op. cit., 390.

48. James A. Christenson and Carolyn E. Sachs, "The Impact of Government Size and Number of Administrative Units on the Quality of Public Services," *Administrative Science Quarterly* 25 (March 1980): 89–101.

49. Chicoine and Walzer, op. cit.

50. W. E. Lyons, David Lowery, and Ruth Hoogland DeHoog, *The Politics of Dissatisfaction: Citizens, Services, and Urban Institutions* (Armonk, N.Y.: M. E. Sharpe, Inc., 1992).

51. Note that Illinois relies heavily on independent park districts to provide park and recreation services. Education also tends to be highly "fragmented," even to the point of differentiating provision of elementary and secondary education in some areas.

52. See Roger B. Parks and Ronald J. Oakerson, "Comparative Metropolitan Organization." *Publius: The Journal of Federalism* 23, no. 1 (Winter 1993): 19–39.

53. Lyons, Lowery, and DeHoog, op. cit.

54. Future research should consider intervening variables—mainly institutional—that might condition the effect of jurisdictional fragmentation on public expenditures and thus further specify the relationship. If, for example, there are institutional constraints that inhibit the separation of provision from production (such as legal restraints on intergovernmental contracting), fragmentation would be less efficient. Future research can examine this relationship by specifying more elaborate multi-equation models, in contrast to the single-equation models cited in this chapter.

CHAPTER FOUR: ORGANIZING THE PRODUCTION SIDE

1. Neither one is a metro area as defined by the Census, but rather a central city and its immediate suburbs.

2. See Roger B. Parks and Ronald J. Oakerson, "Comparative Metropolitan Organization and Governance Structures in St. Louis (MO) and Allegheny County (PA)," *Publius: The Journal of Federalism* 23, no. 1 (winter 1993): especially 21–30.

3. In 1984, there were twenty-two municipalities with fewer than 1,000 residents in St. Louis County. Twenty-one of these municipalities reported provision of police protection, but only one maintained a full-time police department, while two others employed part-time officers. Eighteen of these municipalities contracted out for police protection. In the 1,001–2000 population range, five out of fourteen municipalities contract out while the remainder maintain their own departments. Only a single municipality with a population of more than 2,000 people contracts out for policing.

4. Elinor Ostrom, Roger B. Parks, and Gordon P. Whitaker, *Patterns of Metropolitan Policing* (Cambridge, Mass.: Ballinger Publishing Co., 1978).

5. Because the state has superior legal authority, the relationship between state and county is not necessarily an equal partnership. Allegheny County, for example, has found that its street jurisdiction has gradually become more fragmented (literally) due to state preemption, arguably adding to its costs. In effect, the county has become the residual street provider/producer, picking up the pieces that others—both the state and municipalities—leave behind.

6. Elinor Ostrom, Roger B. Parks, and Gordon P. Whitaker, *Patterns of Metropolitan Policing* (Cambridge, Mass.: Ballinger Publishing Co., 1978).

7. Ibid.

8. See Vincent Ostrom and Elinor Ostrom, "A Behavioral Approach to the Study of Intergovernmental Relations," *Annals of the American Academy of Political and Social Science* 359 (May 1965): 137–146.

9. See R. H. Coase, "The Nature of the Firm," *Economica* 4 (1937): 386–485.

10. See Gordon Tullock, *The Politics of Bureaucracy* (Washington, D.C.: Public Affairs Press, 1965). Coordination costs within an organization also vary with the heterogeneity of the work to be coordinated. Because large public bureaucracies combine the production of service components that have quite different production functions and exhibit variable economies of scale, the difficulty of the task for central coordinators is magnified.

11. See Donald P. Warwick, *A Theory of Public Bureaucracy* (Cambridge: Harvard University Press, 1975).

12. ACIR, *Metropolitan Organization: The St. Louis Case,* 57.

13. Measured by number of sworn officers per capita or expenditures per capita.

14. ACIR, *Metropolitan Organization: The St. Louis Case,* 59.

15. ACIR, *Metropolitan Organization: The Allegheny County Case,* 43.

16. Roger B. Parks, "Metropolitan Structure and Systemic Performance," in *Policy Implementation in Federal and Unitary States,* eds. Kenneth Hanf and Theo A. J. Toonen (Dordrecht, The Netherlands: Martinus Nijhoff), 1985, 161–191.

17. Social capital is formed as individuals contribute voluntarily to one another's welfare. Over time, this creates a tradition of reciprocity that shapes individual expectations and generates trust. On the theory of social capital formation see James S. Coleman, "Social Capital in the Creation of Human Capital," *American Journal of Sociology* 94 Supplement: S95-S120.

18. In one of the most detailed studies, a time-series analysis of the 1967 merger of Jacksonville with Duval County, Florida, concluded that consolidation failed to reduce either tax or expenditure levels. J. Edwin Benton and Darwin Gamble, "City/County Consolidation and Economies of Scale: Evidence from a Time-Series Analysis in Jacksonville, Florida," *Social Science Quarterly* 65 (March 1984): 190–198.

CHAPTER FIVE: METROPOLITAN GOVERNANCE—WITHOUT METROPOLITAN GOVERNMENT

1. Other rules, more akin to price regulation, limit the degree to which local citizens can choose to organize and tax themselves to provide local services.

2. Local governments are frequently characterized as "creatures of the state." This is literally true, however, only in the case of local governments that have special-act

charters. General enabling legislation supplies a set of rules that allows local communities to create local governments. See Ronald J. Oakerson and Roger B. Parks, "Local Government Constitutions: A Different View of Metropolitan Governance," *The American Review of Public Administration* 19, no. 4 (December 1989), 279–94.

3. Joseph F. Zimmerman reported in 1983 that only Alabama, Kentucky, and Virginia did not permit municipalities to frame their own charters. See Joseph F. Zimmerman, *State-Local Relations: A Partnership Approach* (New York: Praeger, 1983), 26.

4. See ACIR, *Measuring Local Discretionary Authority*, M–131, November 1981.

5. Dillon's Rule, a rule of judicial interpretation frequently cited in relation to local governments, requires that all local authority be strictly construed and that doubts be resolved against the local government claiming authority to act. To the extent that home rule allows for local determination of authority through a local charter, the restrictive effect of Dillon's Rule is ameliorated.

6. "The simple but concurrent majority approval requirement may make the consolidation more difficult to achieve than a referendum with approval by a majority of the combined electorate in the jurisdictions affected. Yet the Commission believes that concurrent majority approval gives added assurance to the residents of each city, town, or township that they will not be unwillingly included in a consolidated government and provides a salutary political basis for launching a new municipality." ACIR, *State and Local Roles in the Federal System*, A–88, April 1982, 449.

7. ACIR, *Metropolitan Organization: The St. Louis Case*, 1988.

8. The study of local-government constitutions is in its infancy. Although scholars have long described and classified state rules pertaining to local governments, the effort to understand each state's rules as a constitutional configuration and estimate its impact on patterns of provision and production has barely begun. Counting the number of units of various types does not indicate whether a local public economy is structurally distorted. Only a research program of comparative institutional analysis that examines the "rules of the game" in relation to the strategies chosen by participants can explain the patterns of local government that have been created and generate an empirical basis for evaluation.

9. Technically, boundaries that are too small fail to internalize the potential externalities associated with service provision; some benefits spill over to others. The spillover problem is never completely resolved. Sometimes provision units attempt to convert symbolic boundaries into physical barriers, e.g., fences, walls, or dead-end streets. As long as there are local-government boundaries, nevertheless, there will be spillovers. The size of the benefit spillover relative to total provision diminishes, however, with the increasing size of a provision unit. At some point, spillovers become economically insignificant.

10. The "Chinese box" imagery is used by Robert A. Dahl, *After the Revolution: Authority in a Good Society* (New Haven: Yale University Press, 1970).

11. Little empirical work has been done on the effects of different rules. Martin and Wagner, in a study of the effects of boundary commissions in California, concluded that the introduction of greater restrictions on processes of provision unit formation tend to increase local government expenditures. See Dolores T. Martin and Richard E. Wagner, "The Institutional Framework for Municipal Incorporation: An Economic Analysis of Local Agency Formation Commissions in California," *Journal of Law and Economics* 21 (October 1978). Similarly, Dilorenzo found that restrictions in the growth of special districts in California and Oregon resulted in higher expenditures in selected service areas as compared to states experiencing a rapid growth in special districts. See Thomas

Dilorenzo, "The Expenditure Effects of Restricting Competition in Local Public Sector Industries," *Public Choice* 37 (1981): 569–578.

12. See ACIR, *State and Local Roles in the Federal System*, A–88, April 1982, 396. Voters have approved only some 20 percent of known city-county consolidation proposals since 1921, with the success rate declining.

13. It should not be inferred that suburbs necessarily lack diversity. St. Louis County, for example, is highly diverse with respect to street patterns, housing type, lot sizes, median incomes, commercial development—all of the variation that gives a city its interesting geographic texture.

14. ACIR, *Governmental Structure, Organization, and Planning in Metropolitan Areas*, A–5, July 1961, 39–41.

15. The most recent Commission statement is found in ACIR, *State and Local Roles in the Federal System*, A–88, April 1982, 445. An earlier statement was included in ACIR, *Fiscal Balance in the American Federal System*, vol. 2, Metropolitan Fiscal Disparities, A–31, October 1967, 14.

16. The ten states and years of adoption are as follows: Minnesota, Wisconsin, Alaska—1959; California, Colorado, New Mexico—1965; Washington, Nevada—1967; Michigan, 1968; and Oregon, 1969. This information was reported by Joseph F. Zimmerman in 1983. See Zimmerman, op. cit., 110–120.

17. Ronald C. Cease, *A Report on State and Provincial Boundary Review Boards* (Portland, Oregon: Portland State College, 1968). Cited in Zimmerman, op. cit., 119.

18. David L. Chicoine and Norman Walzer, *Governmental Structure and Local Public Finance* (Boston: Oelgeschlager, Gunn & Hain, 1985), 215.

19. Dolores T. Martin, *Institutional Barriers in the Local Government Market: Effects on Efficiency and Monopoly Power*, Ph.D. Dissertation, n.d. See also Martin and Wagner, op. cit.

20. See Recommendation 3 in the Appendix.

21. ACIR, *Metropolitan Organization: The St. Louis Case*, 1988.

22. Ibid.

23. ACIR, *Metropolitan Organization: The Allegheny County Case*, 1992.

24. See, for example, Ted Robert Gurr and Desmond S. King, *The State and the City* (Chicago: The University of Chicago Press, 1987).

25. Daniel J. Elazar, *Cities of the Prairie: The Metropolitan Frontier and American Politics* (New York: Basic Books, 1970) and *American Federalism: A View from the States*, 2d ed. (New York: Thomas Y. Crowell, 1972), 183–192.

26. Elazar (1972), op. cit., 185.

27. Roger B. Parks and Ronald J. Oakerson, "Comparative Metropolitan Organization," *Publius: The Journal of Federalism* 23, no. 1 (winter 1993): 19–39.

28. Elazar (1972), op. cit., 185.

29. See Parks and Oakerson, op. cit.

30. Charles M. Tiebout, "A Pure Theory of Local Expenditure," *Journal of Political Economy* 44 (October 1956): 416–424.

31. See Barbara H. Moore (ed.), *The Entrepreneur in Local Government* (Washington, D.C.: International City Management Association, 1983).

32. This argument is spelled out in Ronald J. Oakerson and Roger B. Parks, "Citizen Voice and Public Entrepreneurship: The Organizational Dynamic of a Complex Metropolitan County," *Publius: The Journal of Federalism*: 18, no. 4 (fall 1988): 91–112.

33. See ACIR, *Metropolitan Organization: The St. Louis Case*, 1988.

34. Large sections of unincorporated St. Louis County have been developed for a number of years without an incorporation movement arising. One has to assume satisfaction with the homogeneous, but fairly low, service levels county government provides in these areas. On the other hand, incorporation and municipal annexation movements have arisen (and achieved mixed success) in some parts of the county. County government may find it difficult to vary its level of service provision from one part of the county to another. But particular communities that become dissatisfied have alternatives available. See ACIR, *Metropolitan Organization: The St. Louis Case*, 1988.

35. *City and State*, July 1987, 6.

36. Salim Muwakkil, "Breaking Away: Growing Debate on Black Autonomy," *In These Times* (November 11–17, 1987): 7.

37. Ibid.

38. Excellent overview discussions of equity issues in both an interjurisdictional and an intrajurisdictional context are found in Astrid E. Merget and Renee A. Berger, "Equity as a Decision Rule in Local Services," in *Analyzing Urban-Service Distributions*, ed. Richard C. Rich (Lexington, Mass.: Lexington Books, 1982), 21–44 and Elinor Ostrom, "The Social Stratification-Government Inequality Thesis Explored," *Social Science Quarterly* 19 (September 1983): 91–112.

39. Equity can be defined, with Aristotle, as equal treatment of equals and unequal treatment of unequals. The key to equity is proportionality, not strict equality.

40. See John Rawls, *A Theory of Justice* (Cambridge: Harvard University Press, 1971).

41. See especially ACIR, *Fiscal Balance in the American Federal System*, vol. 2, Metropolitan Fiscal Disparities, A–31, October 1967.

42. Mark Schneider and John R. Logan, "Fiscal Implications of Class Segregation: Inequalities in the Distribution of Public Goods and Services in Suburban Municipalities," *Urban Affairs Quarterly* 17 (September 1981): 23–37.

43. Income is not, of course, entirely adequate as a measure of fiscal capacity because of the tax resources represented by commercial and industrial property. The effect of introducing this additional variable, however, would probably not tend to enhance the revenue potential of the very rich relative to the very poor.

44. In fact, a U-shaped curve was observed relating income class to revenues and expenditures, as both the very poor and the very rich outspent middle income municipalities. Breaking down expenditures by function, the very poor spent a great deal more on social services than either middle-income municipalities or the very rich; but the very poor also spent somewhat more on "common functions" than did middle-income communities, though not as much as the very rich. (Seven "common functions" are used in this study: general control, general government, highways, police, fire, parks and recreation, and sanitation.) In terms of total revenues and expenditures, very poor municipalities tended to be brought up to the standard of the very rich, or better, by intergovernmental transfers. In terms of spending on common municipal services, the very poor were brought up to the standard of the "middle class," or better. It should be recognized that even these levels of expenditure might not meet a standard of *compensatory* spending designed to bring standards of living in very poor communities up to some minimum. No data is available using such a standard. The intergovernmental transfers taken into account do not, however, include federal and state transfer payments to individuals and families living in these communities.

45. Schools are included only when they are a municipal responsibility. Usually schools are funded separately.

46. ACIR, *Significant Features of Fiscal Federalism, 1987 Edition*, M–151, June 1987, 57.

47. See ACIR, *Metropolitan Organization: The St. Louis Case*, 1988.

48. Similar findings emerged from ACIR's study of Allegheny County outside Pittsburgh. See ACIR, *Metropolitan Organization: The Allegheny County Case*, 1992.

49. J. C. Weicher, "The Allocation of Police Protection by Income Class," *Urban Studies* 8 (October 1971): 207–220; Robert L. Lineberry, *"Equality and Urban Policy: The Distribution of Municipal Public Services* (Beverly Hills: Sage Publications, 1977); Kenneth Mladenka, "Serving the Public: The Provision of Municipal Goods and Services," Ph.D. Dissertation, Rice University (1974) and "The Distribution of Urban Police Services," *Journal of Politics* 40 (February 1978); P.F. Nardulli and J. M. Stonecash, *Politics, Professionalism, and Urban Services: The Police* (Cambridge, Mass.: Oelgeschlager, Gunn & Hain 1981).

50. G. E. Antunes and J. P. Plumlee, "The Distribution of an Urban Public Service: Ethnicity, Socioeconomic Status and Bureaucracy as Determinants of the Quality of Neighborhood Streets," *Urban Affairs Quarterly* 13 (March 1977): 313–332.

51. Frank S. Levy, Arnold J. Meltsner, and Aaron Wildavsky, *Urban Outcomes* (Berkeley: University of California Press, 1974).

52. Ibid.

53. See, for example, M. T. Katzman, *The Quality of Municipal Services, Central City Decline, and Middle-Class Flight*, Research Report R78–1 (Cambridge, Mass.: Harvard University, Department of City and Regional Planning, 1978); R. A. Berk and A. Hartman, *Race and District Differences in Per Pupil Staffing Expenditures in Chicago Elementary Schools, 1970–1971* (Evanston, Illinois: Northwestern University, Center for Urban Affairs, 1971).

54. See ACIR, *The States and Distressed Communities: The Final Report*, A–101, November 1985.

55. The Minneapolis-St. Paul arrangement, adopted by Minnesota statute in 1971, provided that municipalities in the metropolitan area would share 40 percent of the area's future growth in commercial-industrial property assessments. The ACIR recommended in 1985 that other states consider the adoption of similar tax-base sharing arrangements in "densely settled" areas. See ACIR, *The States and Distressed Communities: The Final Report*, A–101, November 1985, 251–253.

56. The ACIR has long advocated diversification of the local revenue base to include sales and income taxes, as well as property taxes and user charges. See ACIR, *Local Revenue Diversification: Income, Sales Taxes and User Charges*, A–47, October 1974. A common assumption has been, however, that diversification does nothing to alleviate—and may even exacerbate—fiscal inequities. Limited evidence is now being generated to the contrary. A recent study of the seven-county Minneapolis-St. Paul area finds only a slight positive correlation between per capita taxable sales and per capita assessed valuation among cities. At the same time, "Stronger but still moderate correlations were found between sales tax bases and both per capita property tax levies and mill rates." This suggests that the use of a city sales tax would tend to mitigate interjurisdictional fiscal disparities, even though there is a wide variation in sales tax base among cities in a metropolitan area. See J. H. Fonkert, "Local Revenue Diversification in Minnesota, *Minnesota Tax Journal* 2 (winter 1986).

57. See ACIR, *Fiscal Disparities: Central Cities and Suburbs, 1981*, An Information Report, August 1984.

58. David Rusk, *Cities Without Suburbs*, 2d ed. (Washington, D.C.: Woodrow Wilson Center Press, 1995).

CHAPTER SIX: THE CIVIC METROPOLIS

1. See the discussion of "How Much Differentiation Is Enough" in chapter 3.

2. Controlling for demand does not directly measure efficiency, which would require a measure of service output sensitive to quality. The basis for the inference is the assumption that wealthier communities with higher service demands would be willing and able to pay for increased service levels, in terms of both quantity and quality.

3. See Ronald J. Oakerson and Roger B. Parks, "Citizen Voice and Public Entrepreneurship," *Publius: The Journal of Federalism* 18, no. 4 (fall 1988): 91–112.

4. Albert O. Hirschman, *Exit, Voice, and Loyalty* (Cambridge: Harvard University Press, 1970).

5. Ronald J. Oakerson and Roger B. Parks, "Citizen Voice and Public Entrepreneurship," *Publius: The Journal of Federalism* 18, no. 4 (fall 1988): 98.

6. Tiebout himself joined in stressing this mode of competition in Vincent Ostrom, Charles M. Tiebout, and Robert Warren, "The Organization of Government in Metropolitan Areas: A Theoretical Inquiry," *American Political Science Review* 55 (December 1961).

7. ACIR, *Metropolitan Organization: The St. Louis Case*, 1988.

8. See Robert H. Bates, "Macropolitical Economy in the Field of Development," in *Perspectives on Positive Political Economy*, eds. James E. Alt and Kenneth A. Shepsle (Cambridge: Cambridge University Press, 1990), 53.

9. For a more thorough discussion of rural governance, see Ronald J. Oakerson, "Structures and Patterns of Rural Governance," in *The Changing American Countryside: Rural People and Places*, ed. Emery N. Castle (Lawrence, Kans.: University Press of Kansas, 1995), 397–418.

10. A wide-ranging discussion of decentralization issues in the developing world can be found in Elinor Ostrom, Larry Schroeder, and Susan Wynne, *Institutional Incentives and Sustainable Development: Infrastructure Policies in Perspective* (Boulder; Westview Press, 1993).

11. For a discussion of issues concerning tax policy and local fiscal constitutions, see Roger B. Parks and Ronald J. Oakerson, "Local Taxes, Spending, and Public Accountability: How Wisconsin Compares" (Milwaukee: Wisconsin Policy Research Institute, 1990).

12. Although true experimental conditions are lacking, results consistent with theoretical predictions lend support to the theory, especially if contextual variables can be monitored even though not controlled.

13. See also the work of Kathryn A. Foster and her colleagues in the Governance Project at the State University of New York at Buffalo. Their 1996 report *Governance in Erie County: A Foundation for Understanding and Action* is a model of good applied research, combining theoretical sophistication, empirical generalization, and local knowledge.

14. DuPage Intergovernmental Task Force, "Inside DuPage County: Structure and Performance," Summary report of the DuPage Intergovernmental Task Force, 1992.

INDEX

ABOUT THE AUTHOR

RONALD J. OAKERSON (Ph.D., Indiana University) is professor of political science and chair of the Department of History and Political Science at Houghton College. From 1985 to 1988 he was a senior analyst with the U.S. Advisory Commission on Intergovernmental Relations and directed the Commission's research program on metropolitan governance. Previously he taught at Marshall University, and from 1988 to 1992 he was a senior scholar with the Workshop in Political Theory and Policy Analysis at Indiana University, Bloomington.

A former member of the Panel on Common Property Resource Management of the National Research Council, Oakerson coedited *Making the Commons Work: Theory, Practice, and Policy*, published by ICS Press in 1992. Active in international consulting, he served as research director of the Program of Research on Market Transitions for the U.S. Agency for International Development in Cameroon between 1992 and 1994.

Oakerson, a founding member of the National Rural Studies Council, currently serves on the American Political Science Association's Task Force on Civic Education for the Next Century. At present, with support from a grant by the Lynde and Harry Bradley Foundation, he is writing a new introduction to American government, *Keepers of the Republic: A Civic View of American Politics*, forthcoming from ICS Press.

ABOUT ICS

Founded in 1974, the Institute for Contemporary Studies (ICS) is a non-profit, nonpartisan policy research institute.

To fulfill its mission to promote self-governing and entrepreneurial ways of life, ICS sponsors a variety of programs and publications on key issues including education, entrepreneurship, the environment, leadership, and social policy.

Through its imprint, ICS Press, the Institute publishes innovative and readable books that will further the understanding of these issues among scholars, policy makers, and the wider community of citizens. ICS Press books include the writings of eight Nobel laureates, and have been influential in setting the nation's policy agenda.

ICS programs seek to encourage the entrepreneurial spirit not only in this country, but also around the world. They include the Institute for Self-Governance (ISG) and the International Center for Self-Governance (ICSG).